DEDICATION

To my Husband,

Bill

For driving our little economy rental car down all those dusty dirt roads in search of isolated tels, you deserve a medal.

Thank you for indulging my love of the Bible and adventure. Instead of relaxing on your days off, you used some of them to take me exploring.

Although you did not write this book, your insight is sprinkled here and there among its pages. I am so glad that you love Jesus and His Word with all your heart! Your wisdom and understanding have enriched my relationship with God.

As we have walked ancient paths together, Jesus has blessed our efforts to learn more about Him and His Word. I am happy to walk beside you as we love and serve our God.

I love you!

SPECIAL THANKS

Gary and Linda Reed

Thank you for reading the manuscript
and for giving us the opportunity to work with you in Jordan.

Robert and Beth McFarland

Thank you for entrusting us to oversee the
International Biblical College of Jerusalem.

Shadi and Ibtissam Azar

As native Jordanians,
you were highly qualified to review the manuscript.
I greatly appreciate your insight and suggestions.
Ibtissam, for the many Arabic lessons… Shukran jazeelan!

CONTENTS

The Journey

THE BEGINNING OF MY JOURNEY

For as long as I can remember, the Bible has been a part of my life. As a child, I read story books and comic books that depicted popular Bible stories. Soon I graduated to reading the Bible for myself, without the aid of pictures and comic strips.

In my teen years, I discovered that people had written special encyclopedias, dictionaries, commentaries, and atlases to aid people in their personal study of the Bible. I started using some of these study books.

Then, I happened upon a book about manners and customs of Bible times. I was captivated. Here was a book that told the story behind the story. It revealed customs of a bygone day. It explained parables that made little sense to me. It illuminated to me the meaning of phrases that would have been familiar to generations that lived thousands of years ago but had no apparent relevance to me and my generation.

Although my memory did not retain all the tidbits I gleaned from that first book about manners and customs of Bible times, perusing it birthed in me a desire to dig even deeper into the Word. Much can be gleaned from casual reading of the Word. But there are many precious gems hidden just below the surface, pleading for discovery. As I began to study, as well as read, I learned that when I combined prayer with my Bible reading and study, God blessed me and illuminated my mind to deeper things in His Word.

The Word of God is treasure that we store in our hearts and minds. When times of crisis confront us or we are standing at a crossroads, we can draw from this valuable resource. The Word will never mislead us. Without the Word, our lives have no constant, no anchor, no direction...no purpose. And the more Word we have hidden within us, the more ammunition we have to fight temptation, doubt, and discouragement.

So I was hooked, addicted to this inexhaustible, always fresh, book we call the Bible. As the years went by, life seemed to speed up and my time for personal Bible study sometimes waned. Yet, the desire to learn never left me.

THE TURNING POINT

Then, the most unexpected opportunities came our way, and these opportunities dramatically expanded my understanding of Bible manners and customs.

My husband and I received invitations to work in the Middle East – the land of the Bible. After much prayer, we sensed that God was directing us to accept these invitations.

During our assignments in the Middle East, I work alongside my husband, as he ministers in Christian churches and oversees a biblical college. The work requires that we expand beyond our usual limits. It is often difficult and always unpredictable. It stretches us and forces us to grow, to change, and to learn new skills.

Due to language barriers, cultural differences, unfamiliar food, challenging housing situations, and local customs, living in a foreign country can be frustrating. Add in the fact that this area of the world is turbulent and has the potential to become a war zone overnight, and the pressure increases. To help ensure our safety, we are careful to follow the guidance of our leaders and use discretion in our day-to-day life.

Yet, in spite of the difficulties, we consider ourselves immeasurably blessed to teach international groups that love God and His Word. I have accumulated wonderful memories of God ministering to these precious people. As we give, we receive so much more in return, for our lives are blessed to be able to minister to people who crave to know God better.

And as an additional bonus, we find ourselves immersed in a culture so like that of Bible days that it is astonishing. It is a path I never dreamed I would walk. Never once did I imagine that I would live in the land that Abraham sought or visit ruins of cities where Jesus lived and taught.

To me, this is not a dream come true, because I never dreamed of such a thing. To simply visit for a short time would have been my dream come true. But God's plan was to send us to the Middle East, to work and minister.

The land of the Bible. Where it all began. It is where I live, work, shop, eat, sleep.

When in Amman, Jordan, we frequently pass Citadel Hill. This is where noble Uriah the Hittite was killed. When we visit people in their homes, we are given a biblical lesson in hospitality, since their hospitality reflects that of Bible days. When in Jerusalem, we walk through the crooked streets of the Old City for exercise, gazing upon the Mount of Olives and looking down into the Valley of Hinnom.

Simply by living and working day after day in this place-like-no-other, we glean, absorb. History surrounds us; we cannot avoid it. Even when running a menial errand, we learn. The culture itself is a chalkboard filled with 6,000-year-old lessons. We live among people with customs similar to those of the patriarch Abraham, King David, and the prophet Elijah.

History is no longer confined to high school history lessons read from a flat and one-dimensional textbook. It comes alive. A state-of-the-art modern building might be on the site of an ancient battle. Here, the present is so intertwined with the past that wherever I walk, history is never far away.

TRAVELING BACKWARDS

Imagine a world without cars, airplanes, and motorcycles. Imagine a day when there were no computers, mass-produced books, social media, and telemarketing. No high school diplomas and PhDs. No hospitals, fire departments, and border patrol. Forget dishwashers, microwave ovens, refrigerators, indoor plumbing and on-demand hot water. No dating and very little divorce. Consider life without Congress, voting booths, and the United Nations.

Other than the predictability of human nature, there is little about our Western way of life that resembles the way people lived during Bible times. Often, when Westerners read the Bible, we are puzzled by terminology, geography, customs, mindsets, and events that we cannot relate to. We do not understand the culture of the Bible, so we sometimes misinterpret a parable or fail to understand a strange story. We look at the Bible through American eyes and often draw erroneous conclusions as a result.

Bruce Feiler wrote, "There are many dangers in discussing the Bible in contemporary terms; so much about the ancient world bears little resemblance to our democratic, post-Enlightenment world."[1]

I grew up in the United States. So, before I lived in the Holy Land, when I read the Bible, I had only the terrain, climate, and culture of my own country as a frame of reference. As a result, I imagined that the Sea of Galilee must resemble the Lake of the Ozarks. Like most people, I concluded that Martha must have been terribly unspiritual, because my concept of a woman's role in society was shaped by life in modern America. I thought Jerusalem must have been a sprawling metropolis.

But the Sea of Galilee is not enormous and it is not particularly majestic. Martha was actually doing what was good and proper. She loved Jesus; she just needed to realize that sometimes God's customs override man's customs. And ancient Jerusalem was so small that I wondered where Solomon housed all of his wives and concubines!

The reason we have difficulty relating to people from Bible times is because their way of life was so different from ours. From our point of view, their lifestyle seems foreign and archaic. Words like "threshing" and "winnowing" were important to them, because threshing and winnowing were components in the process that eventually turned grain into bread. Today, most of us simply make a quick jaunt to the grocery store to get our bread.

It is interesting to consider that when these people were alive, *they* were the modern ones! I can almost hear Gideon talking to a friend: "Hey, Simeon, check out these pitchers. They are the newest design, made to order for my wife to carry water in. Too bad we will have to break them during our upcoming battle with the Midianites. Oh well, maybe she will not be too upset with me if I buy her some more new pitchers...plus that new pair of sandals she has been wanting!"

Today, we simply turn on our faucet and we get instant water. In Bible days, obtaining water was often an arduous task, relegated to the wives and daughters in the family. They carried water and other liquids in clay or leather jars. Making these jars, or pitchers, was also a labor intensive project. And there were no mega-shoe stores in which to select that perfect pair of sandals, in just the right shade of blue.

In many ways, present Middle Eastern culture mirrors the customs and lifestyles of biblical people as far back as the patriarch Abraham. For thousands of years, little has changed. Family structure, the role of women, the way people communicate, even the way meals are served is like stepping back in time to a world vastly different from the one in which I was raised. Though many Bedouin Arabs have traded desert life for city life, their mentality remains the same. They are tribal and live according to thousands of years of traditional ways of life.

Some people fail to understand how the Bible is relevant to their lives, their problems. Maybe you have wondered, "How can such an old book help me? It uses unfamiliar words and talks about things I cannot relate to."

But in many ways, the people who lived 2,000, 3,000, 4,000 years ago faced the same challenges that we face. Their societies were challenged by complex problems such as racial strife, hatred, murder, adultery, and greed, just as ours is. Human nature has always been the same. The individuals in the Bible were people just like us. They faced the same problems in their families and societies. The Bible is not a book about perfect people. It is a book about a perfect God.

Once we understand the customs and challenges of Bible people, the culture of the nations around them, and the geography of the area, we better understand the people themselves, their struggles, their political loyalties, and so much more. Such knowledge provides us with important insight and gives us a valuable frame of reference.

DIGGING DEEP INTO THE PAST

When overseas, I take a lot of photographs and scribble down copious notes. I read travel guides and articles about archaeological sites. I carefully choose which biblical sites I want to visit. I have minimal interest in sites that are not positively identified as Bible towns. A common phrase in the tourism world of the Holy Land is "according to tradition." This means that there is no true historical evidence to prove that the location is an authentic biblical site.

Much of the controversy about biblical sites is rooted in the actions of Constantine's mother, so-called "Saint" Helena, who visited the Holy Land during the 4th century. She would declare a place to be the location of a key Bible event. She had the power and money to not only establish her word as fact in the religious world, but to order a church built on that site. She claimed to find Jesus' cross and even the nails from it, a piece of His tunic and pieces of the rope that were used to tie Him to the cross.

Yes, I am skeptical, so please direct me to historical sources showing that Helena was properly educated and qualified to make such important decisions. Then I will rethink my opinion of her and her influence in the Holy Land.

So when I know that a site is identified with the Bible "according to tradition," I usually opt to use our time off exploring something more credible. And, when writing, I conscientiously strive to be as factual and accurate as possible.

I like to be off-the-beaten-path anyway. Many people drive or walk by significant places and never even know what they are missing. Most tourists to Israel visit the Temple Mount, the Garden Tomb, the Mount of Olives, the Sea of Galilee and the towns surrounding it. These are wonderful places, and I am sincerely grateful I could visit them, but when it comes to educational sightseeing, I like to be where people are not. It seems people tend to flock to places that are advertised and well-known.

I like to find little hidden gems that connect-the-dots for me biblically or present me with a visual understanding of biblical principles. For example, when I looked down upon the tomb at Ketef Hinnom, the phrase "gathered unto their fathers" made perfect sense. As I sat on a replica of a "Seat of Moses" in an ancient synagogue, I could picture the surroundings as Jesus read from Isaiah and taught the people.

I know some people find it an incredible bore, but I almost get ecstatic when I stand next to a pile of rocks which are the ruins of a biblical city. It is insightful to stand where David, Samson, Nehemiah, and so many others lived, walked, talked, prophesied, and wrote. Seeing the hills that surrounded their villages, or the remains of homes they may have lived in, gives me pictorial background when I read and study the Bible.

Sometimes my husband and I find ourselves all alone on a tel or beside a quiet stream. The solitude enables us to better absorb the meaning of what we are seeing. Since living in the land of the Bible, I even get excited when I read the genealogies!

I am sure that many people who visit the Holy Land, once they return home, are immediately re-immersed into their busy lives. Yes, they were impacted by all they saw, but exactly what did they glean that will help them live for God better than ever before?

Did they glean a thought, a concept that will help them understand an obscure but important Scripture? Did they learn something that they can apply to their own lives, making them better people and helping them have healthier relationships with their family members? Did they learn something from biblical history that will encourage them to change their own personal history, so they do not repeat the mistakes of others?

I would guess that in most cases people simply do not grasp all they could from a trip to the Holy Land. Unforgettable? Yes. Amazing? Yes. But in this book series I want to fill in a few blanks you may have missed when you walked on that celebrated soil. Or, if you have never been to the Holy Land, I share with you some nuggets I found along the way, as I was passing through the land that Jesus walked.

This book, the first of a series, is by no means comprehensive. I do not have a team of experts working with me as I study and I do not consider myself a great scholar. What I offer you is a unique quilt composed of beautiful fragments that I have gathered. It is a non-technical layperson's perspective. Using archaeology, history, geography, and of course, primarily, the Bible, I have pieced together a kaleidoscope of biblical life. It is not complete, for there is so much more to learn, but I hope you enjoy it.

If you are making plans to visit the Holy Land, take special note of each "Tip for the Traveler." These tips offer additional insight unknown to many visitors. If you are traveling on your own and are able to personalize your schedule, you might find this information particularly helpful.

Book One is the product of our nearly yearlong residence in Jordan and Israel. I blend my personal experiences from these two countries with historical and biblical information. I offer ideas on how to apply important principles to our lives. These principles are what help us realize how powerfully relevant the Bible really is.

THE DESTINATION

The ruins I visit speak of a long ago day and long ago events. But God still speaks into our hearts and spirits, because He is still alive. There is a deep, deep element in every man, woman, and child that is rarely tapped. But when we open our hearts to God, He speaks to us and meets our needs.

So, above all, this book is intended to help you draw closer to Jesus. If this book ministers only to your intellect, then I have failed. It is not enough to be enlightened intellectually. The Bible was written for our *personal application.*

We should long to grow spiritually and strengthen our relationship with Jesus. Because when all is said and done, absolutely nothing else matters but Him. I want this book to minister to that deep place within your heart that only Jesus can touch.

My goal is not to simply visit places and chalk the visits up as great experiences in this land commonly called the Holy Land. Knowing the Holy One better – better than ever before – is my goal. My experiences and studies are simply a channel, a tool to help bridge the gap between our humanity and His divinity.

Enjoy your journey as you learn more about Jesus and His precious Word. The journey will never end, but this book can help you along the way.

Listen closely as Jesus whispers to you. He is inviting you, beckoning you to follow Him, to know Him, to walk with Him down ancient paths.

Lod

Nearly all visitors to Israel arrive via Ben Gurion International Airport. (David Ben Gurion was Israel's first prime minister.) This airport is located nine miles from Tel Aviv, in a city called Lod. Former names of this airport include Lod Airport and Lydda Airport.

Lod is mentioned in I Chronicles 8:12, Ezra 2:33, and Nehemiah 7:37; 11:35. In the New Testament, the same city is called Lydda (Acts 9:32-42).

Peter visited the saints who lived in Lydda. While he was there, Aeneas was healed of the palsy by Peter's spoken word and people "turned to the Lord."

So, if you ever visit Israel, as you are waiting in line at Customs and Immigration, take a minute to think about where you are. You are standing on or near the site of Old Testament Lod and New Testament Lydda.

This is no ordinary place, this land of Israel. Even the location of the airport is significant. Somewhere under the tarmac might be ruins of the biblical city where Peter, that first great apostolic preacher, walked, talked, and was used of God to perform a miraculous healing.

This is a land far different from any other, where dusty sandals meet tennis shoes, where the past merges with the present. This is the Holy Land where, from the moment you step off the airplane, you are offered a treasure trove of rich Scriptural nuggets.

Tip for the Traveler

In 1996, during highway construction, a third century Roman mosaic floor was discovered in Lod, not far from the airport. (A mosaic is an arrangement of tiny tiles which create a picture that is usually quite ornate.)

When conservationists pieced together the sections of the Lod Mosaic, it stretched to approximately 50 feet long by 27 feet wide. Although, to date, I have been unable to see the mosaic firsthand, I can tell from photographs that this is an exceptional mosaic. It is animal-themed, from birds to dolphins, with a giraffe here and a tiger there.

A museum is being planned on the site, to provide the public an opportunity to view the mosaic. Although the Lod Mosaic was probably not created during biblical times, it is fascinating nonetheless, and gives us a glimpse into the artistic style in place during the early years of Christianity.

I Need a Hero

We had been living in the Arab world only about a month. A friend of ours told us that he wanted to get back into the army, but was having difficulty due to health problems. He said, "Bill, I need to find a wastah."

The word was new to us so he explained the concept. In the Arab world, a wastah is what Westerners might think of when we say, "It's all in who you know." In business arrangements and even everyday life, a wastah comes in handy. This is a person who can be a go-between for you. They can get you to the head of the line, and they cut through red tape.

To a great degree, Americans are protected in Jordan. We have had two incidents in which total strangers – one was a lieutenant in the Army – gave us their phone numbers and told us to call them if we ever needed their help. That is a wastah. And it was a nice feeling knowing that we could call perfect strangers if we were between a rock and a hard place.

Over time, we were blessed with several other people who became wastahs to us. In particular, one wastah helped us renew our visas, a potentially complicated procedure. He also purchased a car battery for us on Friday...the day when all the stores are closed, including auto parts stores. In a land where our total Arabic vocabulary amounted to about 15 words at the time, having a few wastahs came in handy now and then.

I like the idea of wastah, which rhymes with pasta. I suppose that sometimes it is not good, since the power of a wastah can prevail over merit or ability, but for the most part it is a joined-arms, "I'll give you a hand-up" kind of thing.

The concept of wastah brings to mind I John 2:1-2 which says "My little children, these things write I unto you, that ye sin not. And if any man sin, we have an advocate with the Father, Jesus Christ the righteous: And he is the propitiation for our sins: and not for ours only, but also for the sins of the whole world."

The wastah of the Arab world is a life lesson in our limitations and God's abilities. When we mess up, He lifts us up. When our strength is at an end, He invites us to tap His unlimited resources. He is the best kind of wastah.

I am reminded of a story about a little boy who was eating at a restaurant. There were a lot of people at the table and the conversation was loud and lively. The little boy's feet were twisted in his chair and he was stuck. He tried to get someone to help him but no one heard him over all the adult voices.

Finally, the little guy cried out, "I need a hero!" It was so adorably cute that everyone laughed as someone rescued him from his predicament.

That is a wastah. A hero. Someone that helps us when we cannot help ourselves. I have discovered that God is the Wastah of all wastahs …the best Hero of all.

Iraq al-Amir

Drive west through Amman, Jordan, past 8th circle. Maneuver through a village called Wadi al-Seer, then drive about eight more miles, into country so beautiful and quiet that congested Amman seems thousands of miles away.

The hilly countryside is dotted with olive groves. We wait as a shepherdess herds goats down the street. Seemingly unattended vegetables lie alongside the road and children stare as we drive by; not many tourists venture out this way.

Missouri, where I grew up, is known as the Cave State (Think Jesse James' hideout.) With over 5,500 caves in the state and my parents' inclination to take us to really wonderful nature-oriented places, I enjoyed exploring caves. But none of those Missouri caves were as significant to me as Iraq al-Amir, which translates to mean Caves of the Prince. The Prince referenced was Tobiah, one of the famed opponents of Nehemiah. These caves and the surrounding land were the ancestral domain of his family.

Nehemiah returned to Jerusalem to rebuild its walls and gates, with the permission of King Artaxerses I, who supplied Nehemiah with necessary building materials.

Tobiah the Ammonite, Sanballat the Horonite, and Geshem the Arabian were angry about Nehemiah's goal (Nehemiah 2:10). Tobiah and Sanballat were appointed Persian officials and – although Nehemiah had the king's blessing – they employed several strategies to try to defeat Nehemiah's objective:

~ They tried to intimidate him and put fear in his heart (Nehemiah 6:9,19).
~ They accused him of insurrection to the king (2:19).
~ They ridiculed him and demeaned his work (4:1-6).
~ They conspired with others to catch the Jews unarmed. When the Jews became aware of the plan, they prayed and armed themselves. When their enemies realized that the plan was discovered, they abandoned it (4:7-15).
~ They hired a man to advise Nehemiah to enter the temple to protect himself from his enemies. This was not acceptable according to the laws of God. If Nehemiah would have done this, he would have brought a reproach upon his impeccable reputation (6:10-14).
~ They invited him to meet with them in the plain of Ono in the land of Benjamin, about 30 miles northwest of Jerusalem. (Ono is the modern village of Kefr 'Ana, about five miles north of Lydda.) Chances are good that the proposed meeting was not to be a cozy coffee house chat; rather, Nehemiah's enemies wanted to take him prisoner or do him harm (6:1-4).
~ Tobiah was married to a Jewish woman, and he used his family tie to make the men of Judah loyal to him instead of Nehemiah, creating division in Israel (6:17-18).

None of these things caused Nehemiah to lose focus. He kept building the walls that had been broken down and the gates that had been burned with fire. He did not concede to discouragement and opposition. He prayed. He worked. He solved social problems.

Perhaps Tobiah was so antagonistic toward Nehemiah because he knew he had no legitimate right to be involved in Israel's affairs. He was an Ammonite, not an Israelite with a pure and proven lineage (7:61-62; 13:1). Nehemiah plainly told Tobiah, Sanballat, and Geshem that they had "no portion, nor right, nor memorial, in Jerusalem" (2:20).

Eliashib the priest had allowed Tobiah to occupy a spacious room in the temple; Nehemiah discarded Tobiah's belongings (13:4-9).

I completely disagree with one guide book which stated that if I scrambled up to the caves I would "find very little to get excited about: most are malodorous, and there's nothing to see but the view across the fields and a single ancient Hebrew inscription beside one of the cave entrances..."[1] The caves were fascinating and the beautiful hillsides provide one of the prettiest views in Jordan.

Except for the occasional cry of a shepherd, a dog barking, or the distant sounds of people talking, all was quiet around us. It was incredibly easy to imagine how things must have been here approximately 2,500 years ago. Some of the cave walls are blackened from long ago fires. One of the eleven caves is equipped with rock-hewn seats around the perimeter of the room; this cave probably served as a council and fellowship room. The rocky, terraced hillsides are ideal for grazing flocks and growing food.

In another guide book, I had read that there were *two* Aramaic inscriptions with the family name "Tobiad" inscribed in the outer rock walls of the caves, but we had only seen one.

As we were leaving, Bill happened to turn around and see the second one near another doorway. I was like a kid in a candy store, so excited that we spotted the two identical inscriptions.

How long did Tobiah live here? We cannot know. Perhaps this was his childhood playground, the place where his children were born, and a conference center where he hosted area leaders as they gathered and discussed their world affairs. If these caves could speak, what stories they could tell. But the caves and their two simple inscriptions are quiet, unwilling to reveal the secrets of the Tobiad family, urging us to be content with the biblical account of his life.

It is enough to be inspired by Nehemiah's constant refusal to be distracted, discouraged, intimidated, or afraid. He refused to believe the lies – both obvious and subtle – of his enemies. Nehemiah's adversaries tried a variety of strategies in hopes that one of their tactics would catch him off guard. But nothing worked. The walls were erected. The gates were built. Mission accomplished.

Tip for the Traveler

About half-a-mile beyond Iraq al-Amir is Qasr al-Abd (Palace of the [Royal] Servant). This is the unfinished ruins of Hyrcanus' palace. Hyrcanus was a descendant of Tobiah. Qasr al-Abd was constructed on the family estate within view of the ancient caves.

Even in its time-worn and neglected condition, it is plain to see that the palace, built of large hewn rock blocks and adorned with intricate, imposing statues of wild animals, was elegant in its day.

A Bird's Eye View

In the Bible, animals are often used as object lessons to illustrate important principles. As we were walking atop Jerusalem's Old City Walls, we saw a pretty little bird perched on an old strand of wire. If this bird could have talked, maybe she would have shared with us this tidbit of wisdom: "As a bird that wandereth from her nest, so is a man that wandereth from his place" (Proverbs 27:8).

Some people are never happy where they are. They always look for greener grass, which usually proves to be nothing more than a mirage on the horizon. They are on a constant search for satisfaction, peace, and fulfillment.

Looking in different jobs, locations, and relationships, these people find themselves in an incessant state of frustration. The problem is always with the job, the place, or another person...they think. They never look within.

They are wanderers, constantly looking but never finding what they really need.

As a bird that moves away from the security of her nest, they make themselves vulnerable to attack. One misstep can land them in the snare of the fowler. But they are shortsighted; when they move away from the security and benefits of the nest, they envision only the freedom they hope to gain. They view security as restraint. They have an aversion to responsibility and authority figures. They do not want to be obligated to anyone. The elusive promise of an independent life, free of restrictions and boundaries, lures them away and eventually serves as their demise.

If a mother bird decides to wander from the nest, the eggs or the young birds become vulnerable to attack by animals of prey. They are helpless without Mother Bird there to protect them. So it is when people refuse to allow Jesus to heal them and give them peace. Their spiritual instability and unharnessed emotions keep them hopping from place to place, relationship to relationship. They fail to consider the little people, the vulnerable people in their lives – the children – whose emotional and spiritual security they jeopardize by their wandering.

The old saying is "A rolling stone gathers no moss." Some people's lives never take root because they will not stay in one place long enough to get grounded. They have restless spirits; they are unsettled within. They are their own worst enemy…but they do not even realize it.

Tip for the Traveler

I saw the bird that served as the inspiration for this article as we were taking the self-guided Ramparts Walk tour on top of Jerusalem's Old City Walls. The entrance is at Jaffa Gate. For just a few shekels, the walk helps put the city into spatial perspective…and the views are great. Wear safe, comfortable shoes and be prepared to do a lot of walking and climb a lot of steps.

Purim

Purim is the holiday that commemorates Jewish deliverance by the hand of Queen Esther. Many people wear costumes, some of them quite elaborate and unique. While some people pose as Esther, Mordecai, or Haman, others choose roles that have nothing to do with the story of Purim.

Purim is a bit like Halloween without all the diabolical undercurrents. With the exception of a witch or two and a few skeletons, most of the costumes are pirates, princesses, and the like. We even saw one girl dressed up like a bottle of yellow mustard.

The Talmud tells Jews that during Purim they should drink until they cannot tell the difference between Mordecai and Haman. Apparently, Talmudic writers were trying to emulate the banquets of wine that Esther prepared, although Scripture does not explicitly say that anyone present at those banquets was intoxicated (Esther 5:6; 7:2).

Ben Yehuda Street was a mass of people, yelling, singing, and dancing. Every few minutes, someone would throw a firecracker into the crowd and a few girls would scream, adding to the festive chaos. All of the buildings here are made from Jerusalem stone, and since they are so close together, they capture and magnify sound. It was a loud night and, from our apartment, we could hear the sounds of celebration into the early morning hours. To the credit of their good judgment, although we did see more alcohol than usual, most revelers were drinking non-alcoholic beverages.

This holiday is called Purim because Haman cast lots, or Pur, to determine the date when the Jews should be destroyed (Esther 3:7,13; 9:28).

A Jewish friend told us that Purim is celebrated one month before Pesach, or Passover. He said that this is significant. In Passover we see the undeniable, magnificent hand of God working openly. It was a spectacular deliverance. In Purim, we see God working behind the scenes to deliver His people.

The lesson is that, even if God's hand is not clearly visible, we can be assured He has not forgotten us and is still working. Although God is never mentioned in the book of Esther, He is there nonetheless.

Sandstorms

We were driving south through the Arava Desert. Visibility was poor and by the time we arrived in Eilat, our skin and hair were grimy and dirty, even though the windows in the car were up and the vents were closed. This sandstorm was definitely not one of the Middle East's worst; by comparison, really treacherous sandstorms made this one seem tame.

I remember Jean Saad – a British-born Jordanian – talking about sand to depict a point during a teaching session. She said, "There is a lot of sand in this part of the world." And she is right. It seems to be everywhere. In the United States, it is okay to dust only once a week. In the Middle East, if you do not dust nearly every day, big dust bunnies will accumulate under beds and in corners of rooms.

When we first went to Jordan, we stayed with Gary and Linda Reed until we got settled into our own apartment. The breeze was nice, so one day I opened the window. The cleaning lady happened to be there and let me know that an open window was not a good idea. The breeze I was enjoying would bring with it fine, almost imperceptible, dust. It would be everywhere...and she would have to clean it! That was my introduction to how dust creates an annoyance for people who live in modern Middle Eastern homes.

Sometimes the Bible compares multitudes of people to the sand of the seashore. Abraham was promised that his descendants would be as innumerable "as the sand which is upon the sea shore" (Genesis 22:17). God reaffirmed this promise to Jacob, Abraham's grandson, again using sand as an illustration (Genesis 32:12). The final battle of all ages will be a dreadfully spectacular display of troops, "the number of whom is as the sand of the sea" (Revelation 20:8).

Aside from representing vast numbers of people, the Bible uses sand in other contexts also. In Egypt, Joseph stored up so much food that it was "as the sand of the sea" (Genesis 41:49). Solomon's wisdom is compared to the sand on the sea shore (I Kings 4:29). And God's thoughts "are more in number than the sand" (Psalm 139:17-18).

God used sand as an object lesson because people living in the Holy Land would have no question about what He meant. Though the landscape varies dramatically, it is still primarily desert. And desert means sand...a lot of sand, so much sand that no one can measure it.

Biblical people lived with sand, adjusted to its brutal intensity. For them, there were no intercontinental flights available so they could cash in the harsh desert for a cooler locale. The desert was their world. From birth to death, it surrounded them, influenced them, and shaped their lives.

And the Middle Eastern sand is not pleasantly arranged along the beautiful backdrop of a balmy Hawaii-type setting. The sun is ruthless and the temperatures are merciless. Where the desert is flat and punctuated by little more than an occasional acacia tree, dust devils form. In some places the desert land is cragged, impenetrable, and steep, deterring all but the most tenacious individuals. Even where the sand dunes rise and fall, creating a gloriously daunting sight, the desert – not fragile man – commands respect. This is not a place for the faint-hearted.

The lifestyle of Bedouin tribes closely mirrors the lives of biblical patriarchs. When sand swirls around the Bedouin – the people of the desert – they draw their head coverings around their faces for protection. When a severe sandstorm threatens cities, residents are told to stay indoors if they have asthma or other respiratory problems or if they are very young or very old. A person caught unprotected in a sandstorm has little hope of survival, so the long head covering is an essential item of clothing for a Bedouin, the resilient desert dweller.

From my first naive introduction to desert life, as I enjoyed the curtains gently blowing in the dusty breeze, to driving through a genuine sandstorm in Israel's Arava Desert, I have gleaned a fresh respect for and understanding of biblical people. Their lives were not easy, but they thrived, they grew, they learned. They had no choice, no alternatives, no options. God assigned them to life in the desert. End of discussion.

The tendency to ask, "Why?" seems to be imbedded within us Americans. We also ask, "Why me?" We want a logical explanation, a professional analysis that makes sense of our storms.

Job wanted answers also. In the heat of the desert sun, he sought relief from the sore boils, probably black leprosy, that plagued him. The sun's heat somewhat eased his pain but even so, he was driven to scrape himself with shards of pottery. He cried out, "Why, God?"

But God's voice was silent.

After many chapters of analysis and questions, Job got his answer. But it was not the one he wanted. To Job's many questions, God finally replied, "Who is God? Are you God, Job? Who created this world and everything in it? Did you do that, Job? Why don't you stop trying to figure things out and simply trust me?"

In the end, God's ways really were best for Job. God really did know what He was doing. Rarely will we understand the storm or its purpose until it is over.

The most difficult storms to accept are the ones we create ourselves. The 1930s Dust Bowl, a time of drought and severe dust storms, resulted mostly because farmers did not use proper farming techniques. They ravaged the fragile topsoil layers of Oklahoma and nearby states. Essentially, farmers destroyed their own land. The repercussions were devastating. When drought and wind came, it took with it the farmable soil.

But even when we create our own problems, God will still help us. He is overwhelmingly patient and kind. He will help us pick up the pieces of our lives and start anew.

Trust. Do not fight the storm; find the Secret Place and retreat into its shelter. As the Bedouin wraps himself in his garment, protecting himself from the wind and sand, cold and heat, so can we be protected when we submit ourselves to the coverings of our God. It really is not important that we understand the storm; even if we understood it, we are powerless to change it.

Trust. Rest. Retreat into the arms of your Creator.

Jerusalem

It is the most controversial city on Earth. Three major religions – Judaism, Christianity, and Islam – lay claim to it. It is well acquainted with bloodshed and division. Empires have fought for it. Countless soldiers have breathed their final breath under its skies. Attacked many times, it has risen from the ashes again and again and again.

For many, the mention of Jerusalem evokes feelings of loyalty and nostalgia, even from people who have never been there. Gauging by its importance in Scripture, it seems that such feelings are justifiable because truly, Jerusalem (ירושלים) is unlike any other place on the planet.

THE MEANING OF ITS NAME

This city, called "Jerusalem" over 700 times in the Bible, was initially called Salem. The first mention was in relation to Melchizedek, that mysterious, enigmatic priest-king, who ruled this city during the days of Abraham (Genesis 14:18-20; Hebrews 7:1-21).

The most common and simplistic translation of Jerusalem is the "City of Peace." The root word for "salem" is "shalem," which means "whole and complete; peace."

"Jerusalem" creates a beautiful word picture full of promise. When an individual, community, or nation keeps God in the center, they will be whole and complete…at peace.

The Hebrew word for "peace" has an even more profound meaning. A Jewish rabbi expounds on the expressiveness of the Hebrew language and the word "Shalom" (שלום) in particular: "There is absolutely no way that words and idioms can be accurately reflected in a language so totally unrelated to Hebrew as is English. English is as conceptually related to Hebrew, in thought patterns and mental visualizations, as the Japanese language is to the Cherokee language."

"For instance, the Hebrew word Shalom has little in common with its English translation of 'Peace.' Shalom does not have the passive, even negative, connotation of the word 'peace.' Shalom does not mean merely the absence of strife. It is pregnant with positive, active and energetic meaning and association."

"Shalom connotes totality, health, wholesomeness, harmony, balance, success, the completeness and richness of living in an integrated social milieu."[1]

How could it be better stated? The name "Jerusalem" is rich, deeply significant, and full of promise. Teddy Kolleck, Jerusalem's longstanding mayor (1965 to 1993), summed up the vitality of Jerusalem's importance among the Jewish people: "I think Jerusalem is the one essential element in Jewish history. A body can live without an arm or a leg, not without the heart. This is the heart and soul of it."[2]

PEACEFUL NAMES

The Hebrew word for "Peace" was incorporated into many biblical names. Two of the most notable are Absalom and Solomon, both sons of King David.

Absalom means "My father is peace" and Solomon means "Peaceful." Shlomo, a variation of Solomon, is frequently used by modern Israeli parents to name their newborn boys. The translation of Jehovah-Shalom is "The Lord is Peace" (Judges 6:24). Isaiah 9:6 prophesied that the Messiah would be known as the Prince of Peace.

JERUSALEM'S OTHER NAMES

Throughout its long history, Jerusalem was called by multiple names. In addition to Salem, it was known as Jebusi (Joshua 18:16,28) and Jebus (Judges 19:10-11; I Chronicles 11:4-5). Jerusalem was the home of the Jebusites before King David captured the city and made it his kingdom's capital.

Zion, mentioned by name 154 times in the Bible, referred to a particular mountain in Jerusalem, but in time "Zion" came to be used interchangeably with Jerusalem (II Samuel 5:7; I Kings 8:1; Psalm 74:2; 78:68; 132:13; 137:1).

During Roman times, half a century after the destruction of Jerusalem in 70 A.D., Hadrian, the Roman emperor at the time, rebuilt Jerusalem and called it Aelia Capitolina. Eventually, however, the name of the city again became Jerusalem.

In addition to its varied political and historical names, Jerusalem had many descriptive, poetic names as well. Here are some of them:

~ A city of truth (Zechariah 8:3)
~ The holy city (Nehemiah 11:1; Isaiah 52:1; Matthew 4:5)
~ The faithful city (Isaiah 1:21)
~ The city of righteousness (Isaiah 1:26)
~ The joyous city (Isaiah 22:2; 32:13)
~ Ariel (Isaiah 29:1,2,7)
~ A city not forsaken (Isaiah 62:12)
~ City of God (Psalm 46:4; 87:3)
~ Perfection of beauty (Psalm 50:2; Lamentations 2:15)
~ Joy of the whole earth (Psalm 48:2)
~ The throne of the Lord (Jeremiah 3:17)
~ City of the great king (Matthew 5:35)
~ City of Judah (II Chronicles 25:28)
~ City of David (II Samuel 5:7; 6:10,12,16; I Kings 2:10;
   Nehemiah 3:15; 12:37; Isaiah 22:9)

SAYING "JERUSALEM"

Once a week, we traveled on a sherut (a 10-passenger van) from Jerusalem to Tel Aviv. For our journey home, we walked to the Tel Aviv bus station where several sheruts, slated to travel to different destinations, gathered. As we approached, each driver would call out the name of his destination.

At first, we could not understand what the drivers were saying. But eventually, we realized that "Yerushalayim" – pronounced "Yuh roo shuh lah eem" – was where we wanted to go. It is a far cry from the English pronunciation of Jerusalem, but I like it. It is, after all, the correct and more authentic pronunciation of this great city.

GREETINGS OF PEACE

The most common greeting heard in Israel is "Shalom." The Arabic variation is similar: "Salam." What a wonderful way to say "Hello." A frequently heard Arabic greeting is "Salam aleikum." This means "Peace be unto you."

This mirrors the biblical greeting, which Jesus used. "And as they thus spake, Jesus himself stood in the midst of them, and saith unto them, Peace be unto you" (Luke 24:36; John 20:19,26). This meaningful and expressive phrase said so much more than just "Hi."

JERUSALEM'S GEOGRAPHY

Psalm 48:1-2 is a beautiful passage of Scripture: "Great is the LORD, and greatly to be praised in the city of our God, in the mountain of his holiness. Beautiful for situation, the joy of the whole earth, is mount Zion, on the sides of the north, the city of the great King." Jerusalem is approximately 2,550 feet, or half-a-mile, above sea level. The word "situation" literally means "elevation." Literally and figuratively, Jerusalem was elevated.

Psalm 122:3 provides additional clues to Jerusalem's topography: "Jerusalem is builded as a city that is compact together." Then as now, Jerusalem's buildings were arranged in a terraced style, close together. Most of the time, a single wall was the partition for two houses.

Psalm 125:2 also poetically explains how Jerusalem was situated: "As the mountains are round about Jerusalem, so the LORD is round about his people from henceforth even for ever." On three sides, between these mountains, Jerusalem is surrounded by valleys. If you visit, keep in mind that the valleys used to be deeper than they are now. Over time, they have accumulated rubbish and debris from destroyed buildings; in Old Testament times, the ravines were much steeper.

The names of Jerusalem's three valleys will be familiar to Bible readers. The *Kidron Valley* separates the Temple Mount from the Mount of Olives. It is filled with graves. Jesus would have walked across this valley on his way to the Mount of Olives (II Samuel 15:23; I Kings 15:13). The *Valley of Hinnom*, from which the word and idea of Gehenna are derived, was the site of horrendous, idolatrous child sacrifice to the god Molech (Leviticus 18:21; II Kings 23:10; II Chronicles 28:3, 33:6; Jeremiah 7:31; 19:2-6). The third valley is the *Tyropoeon Valley*, which means "Valley of the Cheesemakers." Today, it is called the Central Valley.

JESUS AND JERUSALEM

It is a sorrowful, plaintive lament. "O Jerusalem, Jerusalem, thou that killest the prophets, and stonest them which are sent unto thee, how often would I have gathered thy children together, even as a hen gathereth her chickens under her wings, and ye would not" (Matthew 23:37; Luke 13:34). Here, the Messiah's deep compassion is evident. How He desired to love, to gather, to nourish the people who shared His genealogical roots, people He interacted with...people He cared about.

If only the same thing could never be said of us! As the Lord tries to protect us and gather us under His wings, why should we fight Him? It is better to simply submit to His love and allow Him to hold us and care about us. Some people expend a lot of energy fighting God and His will, never understanding that the only thing He wants to do is help them and love them.

JERUSALEM, A PLACE FOR GOD'S NAME

In Scripture, God's name is inseparably connected with Jerusalem. Many verses explain that God chose Jerusalem out of all the tribes of Israel as a place to put His name. (See Deuteronomy 12:5,11; 26:2; I Kings 8:29; 11:36; 14:21; II Kings 21:4,7; 23:27; II Chronicles 6:6, 12:13; 33:4,7.)

From the start, there was something special about this city, this geographical dot on the globe. God placed His name there. For many years, Jerusalem, its temple, and its inhabitants were the focal point of God's attention.

BEGINNING AT JERUSALEM

In the New Testament there is a shift. Undoubtedly God's heart is still towards Israel, "that they might be saved" (Romans 10:1). But something remarkable happened about 2,000 years ago that changed history.

Luke wrote that "repentance and remission of sins should be preached in his [Jesus'] name among all nations, beginning at Jerusalem." Jesus said to His disciples, "Behold, I send the promise of my Father upon you: but tarry ye in the city of Jerusalem, until ye be endued with power from on high" (Luke 24:47-49).

Obediently, Jesus' disciples waited for this Promise. On the day of Pentecost, a Jewish feast, they received the Promise of the Holy Ghost (Acts 2:1-4). The book of Acts records believers being baptized "in the name of the Lord Jesus" (Acts 2:38; 8:16,36; 10:48; 19:5).

From this point forward, there was a change in how God interacted with mankind. No longer was His blessing and name confined exclusively to the nation of the Jews. No longer did He dwell in temples made with men's hands (Acts 7:48; 17:24). But He would live in the heart of anyone who would receive Him, regardless of nationality.

The events of that notable Day of Pentecost invited everyone to enjoy the blessing of having the name of God – which the New Testament revealed to be Jesus – on their lives through baptism in Jesus' name. And to think, it all began at Jerusalem.

PRAY FOR THE PEACE OF JERUSALEM

It is biblical and right to "pray for the peace of Jerusalem," and its inhabitants. But praying for peace among the body of Christ is also needed.

Galatians 4:26 explains, "Jerusalem which is above is free, which is the mother of us all." In the New Testament, believers were "born again" and became "heirs according to the promise" (Galatians 3:29). "But glory, honour, and peace, to every man that worketh good; to the Jew first, and also to the Gentile: For there is no respect of persons with God" (Romans 2:10-11).

Jerusalem. The City of Peace. Who to better describe it than David, the shepherd-king who loved Jerusalem and the God of Jerusalem. Psalm 122 is one of his songs:

> "I was glad when they said unto me,
> Let us go into the house of the LORD.
> Our feet shall stand within thy gates, O Jerusalem.
> Jerusalem is builded as a city that is compact together:
> Whither the tribes go up, the tribes of the LORD,
> unto the testimony of Israel,
> to give thanks unto the name of the LORD.
> For there are set thrones of judgment,
> the thrones of the house of David.
> Pray for the peace of Jerusalem:
> they shall prosper that love thee.
> Peace be within thy walls, and prosperity within thy palaces.
> For my brethren and companions' sakes, I will now say,
> Peace be within thee.
> Because of the house of the LORD our God
> I will seek thy good."

Tip for the Traveler

Here is a brief list of biblically-related Jerusalem sites that, to date, I have found most educational. I only list sites I have seen firsthand. There are others I was unable to visit. Use this list as a springboard. More information can be found on the Internet, so you can do your own homework to personalize your visit as your interests dictate.

The Old City – Jewish Quarter:
   The Western Wall
   The Western Wall Tunnel
   Ariel Center for Jerusalem in the First Temple Period
   The Cardo
   The Broad Wall
   The Burnt House
   Wohl Archaeology Museum

The Old City – Armenian Quarter:
   St. Mark's Church

Mount Zion

The City of David

The Mount of Olives and the Garden of Gethsemane

Gordon's Calvary and the Garden Tomb

Bloomfield Gardens (Herod's Family Tomb)

The Israel Museum:
   Biblical and Archaeology Wing
   Shrine of the Book
   Model of Jerusalem in the Second Temple Period

Bible Lands Museum

Shabbat

At sundown Friday, a siren sounds to announce the beginning of Shabbat (the Sabbath). Though a few cars and pedestrians still create a little activity, for the most part Jerusalem's streets are quiet. Most shops and restaurants, other than a few non-Kosher ones, are closed until sundown Saturday. It is time for religious observance, family, and rest.

Although it is strange for almost everything to be closed, and inconvenient if you need something from the store, I like the concept of Shabbat as it is observed in Israel. In America, for many people a day off means a time to mow the lawn, go grocery shopping, and take the kids to a ballgame. In our success oriented society, a "rush here, rush there" mentality prevails even when people have time off. These days, many Americans do not even set aside time during their week to worship God and learn from His Word.

For some of us, a mild guilt trip takes over if we are not stressed to the max. In Jerusalem, for the religiously observant, Shabbat is much more than simply a day off. It is a restful intermission. It is pausing in the middle of accomplishment, labor, and life's demands. It is a time to focus on what is most important: God, His precious Word, and our families.

God instituted the Sabbath day in the Old Testament. I see His kindness here, as He considers the importance of rest. Since humans tend to have difficulty maintaining balanced lives, God probably knew that people would overwork themselves, so He created a commandment: "Remember the sabbath day, to keep it holy. Six days shalt thou labour, and do all thy work: But the seventh day is the sabbath of the LORD thy God: in it thou shalt not do any work" (Exodus 20:8-11). He likened the Sabbath to Creation, when He rested on the seventh day.

(Like all the other commandments, this commandment was designed to help and protect people. Unfortunately, many people only view divine commandments as restrictions.)

In the New Testament, Jesus angered the law-conscious Pharisees by His seeming disregard for the Sabbath. To one of their accusations, Jesus responded, "The sabbath was made for man, and not man for the sabbath: Therefore the Son of man is Lord also of the Sabbath" (Mark 2:27-28). This astonished and puzzled the Pharisees, but Jesus was introducing to them a different type of Sabbath.

Hebrews elaborates on this beautiful fulfillment of the Old Testament Sabbath: "There remaineth therefore a rest to the people of God. For he that is entered into his rest, he also hath ceased from his own works, as God did from his." (Hebrews 4:9-10). The word translated into "rest" is a derivative of "Sabbath."

As Christians, we should live in a state of continual spiritual rest and contentment. It is not God's design that we live weighed down with mental stress and chronic anxiety. For us, every day is Shabbat, because Jesus is our rest, our refreshing, and our burden-bearer.

Tel Tamar

On a rare three-day break, we decided to get away from the hustle and bustle of Jerusalem's busy core, where we lived and worked. We headed for Eilat, a modern resort town beside the Red Sea on the site of biblical Elath.

On the way, we stopped at Tel Tamar, located just off Highway 90, about 25 miles south of the Dead Sea (Ezekiel 47:18-19; 48:28). Tamar means "Palm Tree." In this arid land, palm trees are found where there is a water source. Today, biblical Tamar is called Ein Hatzeva. In Hebrew, Ein means "Spring."

It is no wonder that Tamar served as an oasis for travelers passing through this brutal, forbidding desert; in the desert, water is vital for survival.

Tamar served as a way station for an ancient trade and spice route. One layer of ruins revealed that the Nabateans, great traders and the famous architects of Petra, inhabited Tamar for a while. Later, the Romans would occupy Tamar, fortifying it as a desert outpost. A four-room house and a fortress dating to Israelite times have been identified. So far, archeologists have uncovered six strata of civilization at this southern site.

But to me, Tamar's most significant historical link was a heap of broken clay and stone religious artifacts that was found outside one of the city walls. This pile of idols, altars, cups, and incense burners was discovered in 1993.

In the 7th century B.C., an Edomite temple was used here, apparently by Jews who lived in Tamar. The land of Edom is located directly east of Tamar and, like so many times in biblical history, the Jews allowed themselves to be influenced by the religious beliefs of the people who lived close to them.

By all appearances, these ritual vessels and altars were deliberately destroyed and thrown into a pit. Although the Bible does not mention Tamar directly in relation to King Josiah's religious reforms and revival of righteousness, it is highly likely that these idols were destroyed during his reign.

King Josiah was one of Judah's righteous kings. His father Amon and his grandfather Manasseh were evil and worshipped false gods.

But Josiah took a different path. Josiah repaired the house of the Lord. During the renovations, Hilkiah the high priest found the book of the law and sent it to King Josiah. As Josiah listened to the words of the book being read to him, he realized that God was angry with His people because of their great sins. When Josiah humbled himself before God, the Lord told him that He would not administer judgment during Josiah's reign.

Josiah wanted to serve God and he wanted his country to serve God. So he "made a covenant before the LORD, to walk after the LORD, and to keep his commandments and his testimonies and his statues with all their heart and all their soul, to perform the words of this covenant that were written in this book" (II Kings 23:3).

Josiah cleansed the land of idol worship. All of the vessels that were in the House of the Lord that had been used for Baal worship were burned. Josiah went throughout the land, destroying idols, breaking down altars and high places, restoring worship of the God of Israel. II Chronicles 34:7 says, "And when he had broken down the altars and the groves, and had beaten the graven images into powder, and cut down all the idols throughout all the land of Israel, he returned to Jerusalem."

Josiah was thorough when he cleansed the land of idolatry. Although the Bible does not list every place Josiah visited during this purification process, it is highly likely that his campaign extended to Tamar.

The pile of cultic remains found at Tamar is currently being stored in the Israel Museum in Jerusalem. They are testimony to the tendency of humankind to drift from worship of the One True God to the worship of gods made of wood, stone, and clay. Heathen nations believed that their gods caused the ground to be fertile, which meant that there would be plenty of food to eat. They trusted in their gods to deliver them from conquering nations and bring them prosperity.

Why did God get angry when the children of Israel worshipped other gods? He was angry because by their actions they were saying, "God, we do not trust you. We do not think you are able to help us." They allowed themselves to be influenced by the gods of the people around them, gods that were created by men's hands.

There are a lot of lessons for us here, but the ultimate lesson is that we need to continually remind ourselves of the first law of all: There is only one God (Deuteronomy 6:4). Essentially, God said to His people, "Before you learn anything else, learn that I am God and I am the only God. If you forget everything else, do not forget this. I am the only God that you need."

Tip for the Traveler

A tiny moshav (a cooperative Jewish town) called Ir Ovot is a stone's throw away from Ein Hatzeva. It commemorates the biblical city of Oboth, where the Israelites stopped for a while during their wilderness travels (Numbers 21:10-11; 33:43-44). Oboth means "bottles."

I saw a crudely drawn sign advertising a crocodile farm in Ir Ovot, but we were hot, dusty and still a long way from Eilat, so we did not bother the desert crocodiles. (Creatures with long jaws and ferocious-looking teeth are not my favorite thing, anyway.) But if you like crocodiles, plan on a side trip to the farm.

Bethlehem

"Oh little town of Bethlehem, how still we see thee lie…" This traditional Christmas carol evokes soothing images of stillness, peace and rest. The song makes me think of a Thomas Kinkade painting depicting a quaint little Bavarian-style village. Warm light spills from the windows of cozy cottages, beckoning weary travelers, inviting them to be refreshed by the serenity of a perfect world.

In reality, the modern town of Bethlehem has little tranquility to offer. Currently, Bethlehem is a town politically divided. The population of 30,000 is a blend of ethnicities and religions, with Palestinian Muslims now taking the population lead. The constantly shifting political atmosphere produces an unstable environment in Bethlehem. No one – regardless of ethnicity or religion – is insured a safe haven in the not-so-little town of Bethlehem.

Even at the time of Jesus' birth, Bethlehem's inhabitants probably did not live with a sense of perfect security. After all, Herod the Great, an unpredictable and paranoid madman, ruled over their lives. He did not flinch at ordering the slaughter of children in Bethlehem two years and younger, in his attempt to destroy Jesus.

PILGRIMAGE TO BETHLEHEM

I suppose my visit to Bethlehem was a bit jaded from the start. I wanted to visit the town but I had repeatedly been told that Bethlehem was not the dreamy town of manger scenes and cute Christmas plays.

Not only is this historic town rife with political dissent, it is also monopolized by religious groups who cater to tourists' inclination to gravitate to sacred and supposedly-sacred places. Tourists, Christian clerics, Arab merchants, and taxi drivers create quite a colorful, and slightly chaotic, crowd.

Since Jewish rental cars cannot be driven into this Palestinian-controlled area, we took a taxi into Bethlehem. Our pass through the Bethlehem checkpoint was a breeze, thanks to checkpoint personnel who took one quick glance at us and decided we did not look too threatening.

Once in Bethlehem, our taxi driver pulled up to a hotel, not our destination. Turns out he thinks we need a guide…one of his friends. We do not want one but it takes a while to convince them of our decision.

MANGER SQUARE

Manger Square is dominated on one side by the Mosque of Omar and on the other side by the unembellished Church of the Nativity. This church is a hodge-podge blend of architecture. Three different religious orders are allocated space in this building: the Greek Orthodox Church, the Roman Catholic Church, and the Armenian Orthodox Church.

We bent low as we entered through the undersized doorway. The dimly lit, stone-lined central room is supported by Corinthian columns and adorned with various religious icons, wall murals, and garish chandeliers.

A long line had formed to the right. People were waiting their turn to view the traditional place of Jesus' birth. An Arab man approached us. He told us that he was a guide and that if we hired him, he had the authority to get us to the front of the line. We accepted his offer, unaware at the time that he was an *unofficial* guide.

We followed him as he wormed his way into the mass of tourists. Not exactly our idea of winning friends and influencing people, but by this time we were committed. (Live and learn!) Our experience made me think of public grade school children cutting into a long lunch line, eager to get their favorite government-issued meal. Rather than a slice of pizza or sloppy Joes, however, everyone was eager to view the place that Helena, Constantine's mother, declared was the very spot where Mary had given birth to Jesus.

With our "guide" beside us, we followed close behind a group of men in black robes; I assume they were monks. At one point they broke into singing, in Latin, I presume. After inching through a narrow hallway, where wax from overhead candles dripped onto one of my favorite sweaters, we reached our destination.

Over a grotto (cave) that is under the jurisdiction of the Greek Orthodox Church, a 14-pointed star adorns the marble floor of a dimly lit altar. No one seems to know why there are 14 points on the star. The most plausible explanation is that the number 14 represents the three 14-generation segments that link Abraham, David, and Jesus. (See Matthew 1:17).

At this place that allegedly marks Baby Jesus' delivery room, people bent to kiss the star on the floor. We declined the kissing procedure, preferring to view the décor and engage in some people watching.

BETHLEHEM BASICS

Like most of Israel, Bethlehem's buildings are constructed of stone, close together, in a peg-leg style along the sides of hills.

And like many ancient biblical cities, Bethlehem sits atop a winding ridge. The hilly country is green enough for shepherds to keep their flocks supplied with adequate pasture.

Bethlehem is a mere five miles south of Jerusalem. In biblical times, it was within the boundary of the tribe of Judah. At the time when Jesus was born, Bethlehem was not a large town, nor was it a popular destination.

Bethlehem was also called Ephrath (Genesis 35:16), Ephratah (Ruth 4:11), Bethlehem Ephratah (Micah 5:2), Bethlehemjudah (Judges 17:7-9; 19:1; Ruth 1:1-2; I Samuel 17:12), and the City of David (Luke 2:4,11). (Note: Jerusalem was also called the City of David.)

What English-speaking people call Bethlehem is Beit Lechem in Hebrew. It means "House of Bread" and is pronounced "Bet-lekh-em." The Arabic is similar – Bet Lahm – and translates to mean "House of Meat." In the Bible, "bread" and "meat" are often generic words that simply mean "food."

So, the overall meaning of Bethlehem is "House of Food" with an unstated special reference to grain and bread. An example of Bethlehem's grain industry is seen in Ruth 1:22. Ruth and Naomi arrived in Bethlehem in "the beginning of barley harvest."

RACHEL, RUTH, AND DAVID

Several notable Bible figures – Rachel, Ruth, and David – have connections to Bethlehem.

Rachel was Jacob's beloved wife. She was buried near Bethlehem (Genesis 35:19; 48:7). A tomb commemorates her death and women go there to pray for safe pregnancies.

Ruth, a woman from the land of Moab, married a man from Bethlehem who had moved to Moab with his mother, father, and brother to escape a famine in the land of Judah. Apparently, Ruth and her husband were unable to conceive children together. After his death, Ruth traveled the difficult route to Bethlehem with her mother-in-law Naomi, who had also become a widow.

It was in Bethlehem that Ruth married another Bethlehem native, Boaz. Ruth and Boaz were David's grandparents. Ruth and Boaz are also listed in the genealogical account of Joseph, Mary's husband. Since genealogical records were not kept for women, but men only, this provides a legal record of Jesus' earthly ancestral line (Ruth 1:1-22; 4:13; Matthew 1:5; Luke 2:4; John 7:42).

David grew up in Bethlehem. It was here that he was anointed king by the prophet Samuel. It was on the hills of Bethlehem that he guarded his father's sheep, cultivated his ability to use a sling, and killed a bear and a lion to protect the sheep. Samuel, at the command of the Lord, traveled to Bethlehem to anoint David king of Israel (I Samuel 16:1-13).

KING DAVID'S WELLS

One of the more interesting sites in Bethlehem is also one of the most obscure. King David's Wells are three cisterns that were discovered in 1895. They are surrounded by a low metal gate.

Since we did not know that the wells could be reached by walking just a short distance from Manger Square, we opted for the long way. (That seems to be our trend, since we serve as our own tour guide. It is more economical, and we need the exercise anyway!) We climbed up an entire hillside of steps, hurrying since the taxi driver was waiting for us. The wells, which are located on the property of a Catholic school, were deserted. We opened the unlocked gate and let ourselves into the site.

Why are these wells significant? Even though it is unknown if these wells have a biblical connection, it is tempting to imagine heroes from David's army furtively drawing water from one of them.

When David was in hiding, trying to preserve his life from Saul's wrath, he longed out loud for a drink of water from Bethlehem's well: "Oh that one would give me drink of the water of the well of Bethlehem, which is by the gate!"

Then as now, Bethlehem was a city in conflict. The Philistines had invaded the area and taken control of David's hometown, turning it into a battle zone. Three of David's loyal warriors broke through the enemy lines and brought David precious water from the well. David was so overwhelmed by the loyalty and courage of these mighty men, he poured the water out onto the ground (II Samuel 23:14-17; I Chronicles 11:16-19).

BETHLEHEM'S BEAUTY

But to Christians, Bethlehem is best known as the birthplace of Jesus, the Messiah. Micah prophesied His birth: "But thou, Bethlehem Ephratah, though thou be little among the thousands of Judah, yet out of thee shall he come forth unto me that is to be ruler in Israel; whose goings forth have been from of old, from everlasting" (Micah 5:2).

The Wise Men, seeking the King of the Jews, referred to Micah's prophecy when they responded to Herod the Great's inquiry about where this new King would be born: "And they said unto him, In Bethlehem of Judaea: for thus it is written by the prophet, And thou Bethlehem, in the land of Juda, art not the least among the princes of Juda: for out of thee shall come a Governor, that shall rule my people Israel" (Matthew 2:5-6). Here, the word "rule" gives the picture of a shepherd tending and feeding his flock. During His ministry, Jesus would refer to Himself as the Good Shepherd.

In the hills of Bethlehem, shepherding was a common occupation. Today, tourists visit Beit Sahur to view the Shepherds Fields, one of the areas that has historically been a place where shepherds keep their flocks. It is fitting that Jesus was born in such a place. He said, "The good shepherd giveth his life for the sheep" (John 10:11). Just as David jeopardized his life for the sheep, killing a lion and a bear, Jesus also served as the barrier between life and death for the creation He so loves. Unlike David, however, Jesus offered Himself as the ultimate sacrifice, dying so the sheep could live.

Two famous shepherds – David and Jesus – were both born in the House of Bread to bring light and direction to a nation in crisis. As the birthplace of two notable shepherds – earthly King David and heavenly King Jesus – Bethlehem has a justifiable claim to fame.

In Bethlehem, none of the sites visited today can be connected to biblical events with even the slightest accuracy. Nevertheless, Bethlehem is still Bethlehem. It is the place where the Messiah was born. Somewhere nearby angels sang, shepherds rejoiced, and a young mother held her precious newborn baby.

He was Son of man, Son of God. Jesus Christ...the Lamb, the Bread of Life, the Savior of the world. "For unto you is born this day in the city of David a Saviour, which is Christ the Lord" (Luke 2:11).

The Sanhedrin

What we commonly refer to as the Sanhedrin is called "the council" in the New Testament. "The council" is translated from a Greek word (sunedrion) which generally means "Sitting Together."

During Jesus' time, the Great Sanhedrin in Jerusalem was a 71-member group of men that met daily (with the exception of the Sabbath and other holy days) in a room that adjoined the Temple. The Sanhedrin developed during the Intertestamental Period and ceased to have credible power after the destruction of Jerusalem in 70 A.D. In addition to this most powerful Sanhedrin that met at the Temple, each city could have its own smaller Sanhedrin, made up of 23 members. These were called Lesser Sanhedrins.

The Sanhedrin was comprised of chief priests, prominent family members related to the chief priests, scribes (legal professionals), Pharisees, Sadducees, and other qualified elders. Apparently, the head of the Sanhedrin was the High (Chief) Priest.

The Sanhedrin had diverse responsibilities: legislative, judicial, and administrative. These men were experts on religious law. They established and enforced religious and civil order. The Sanhedrin served as a court that resolved issues brought to it by Lesser Sanhedrins.

Jesus (Matthew 26), Peter and John (Acts 4), Peter and the other apostles (Acts 5), Stephen (Acts 6), and Paul (Acts 22-25) were all brought before the council, or Sanhedrin, for questioning and judgment.

Gamaliel was a member of the Sanhedrin (Acts 5:34). It is highly likely that Joseph of Arimathaea and Nicodemus were also part of the council (Mark 15:43; John 3:1).

A Rose-Red City

Johann Ludwig Burckhardt, a young Swiss explorer, was the first Westerner known to view Petra in recent history. In 1812 he traveled to Wadi Araba under the assumed name of Ibrahim ibn Abdullah. At that time, Petra, a maze of ancient rock-hewn temples and tombs, was seen only by Bedouins.

These days, Petra is a popular tourist attraction in Jordan, drawing visitors from near and far. Most of the magnificent sandstone carvings are facades of tombs. Some of them served as banqueting rooms and chambers to perform memorial ceremonies for the dead. Homes and public buildings are still being excavated. Other ruins on the site are from the Roman era, more recent additions to the towering carved rock walls.

I found Petra hauntingly beautiful, a strange place that, if not for the hordes of tourists milling about, would have seemed desolate. It is a natural fortress isolated in the middle of the desert, seemingly a million miles from nowhere.

THE NABATEANS

Little is known of the enigmatic Nabateans. Who were their ancestors? Why did they disappear from the record of history? These mysterious people leave historians and tourists with a lot of unanswered questions. But what we do know forms a picture of an unusual society, most likely comprised of 20,000 to 30,000 residents.

Dates vary, since there is so little history about the Nabateans' move to Petra. It is a wide spread, but it is likely that they began to inhabit Petra between the sixth and third century B.C.

As they developed into a highly sophisticated society, several things set the Nabateans apart from the nations around them. For one, to maintain harmony with others, they employed diplomacy instead of warfare. Also, it was acceptable for women to assume prominent roles in governmental leadership.

Without a doubt, the Nabateans were polytheistic. In Petra is no shortage of niches where statues of gods would have been placed. Altars, including the High Place, indicate that pagan worship was a central part of their lives. And the Nabateans were obsessed with the afterlife; hence, such elaborate burial places.

The success of the Nabateans was due in large part to their ability to store water. They built huge cisterns to catch and contain water during winter's flash floods. The Nabateans created an elaborate water distribution system, strategically carving channels out of the rock.

Apparently, their water engineering system was so good that they had sufficient water to not only bathe and supply households with water, but some people even cultivated vineyards and orchards. Plus, they provided water for the visitors that frequented their city. I read about a stream that flows through the city. I did not notice it, though I might have walked right past it, since it was probably a dry bed during the time we visited.

Petra was located along an ancient trade route, the Kings Highway, and this self-governed city capitalized on its location. Petra became an essential stop for caravans of merchants and traders from places like Egypt, Syria, and India. Some of the trade goods that passed through Petra were cloth, art, incense (especially frankincense), precious metals, and exotic spices. Strabo, a Greek historian, recorded that Nabateans considered financial success so important that unprofitable merchants were fined.

Most modern visitors enter Petra through the Siq, a narrow gorge that continues to taper until the visitor rounds a bend for his first glimpse of the magnificent Al-Khazneh, better known as the Treasury. Visitors to Petra long ago would have also entered this way.

It is said that the Nabateans intentionally carved the Treasury in this location to impress visitors and traders with their prosperity and progressiveness. Especially at that time, the magnificence of such a place would have awed travelers, weary from a long trek through the hostile desert.

For several centuries, Petra was successful at maintaining its political and financial independence. But as sea trade began to replace land routes, Petra's industry fell into decline. Also, Petra was unable to withstand the powerful Roman Empire and capitulated to its rule in 106 A.D. Little is heard of Petra again until the arrival of Burckhardt in 1812.

THE EDOMITES

When describing Petra, most guide books refer only to the Nabateans. As a result, few people know that Petra has some fascinating biblical links that predate the Nabateans. Long before the Nabateans moved into the neighborhood, the Edomites occupied Petra.

Question: Who were the Edomites? Answer: The Edomites were descendants of Esau.

Esau was Isaac's son and Jacob's twin brother. When Esau was born, he had red hair. Of Esau's birth, Genesis 25:25 says, "The first came out red, all over like an hairy garment; and they called his name Esau."

One day, Esau, a skillful hunter, came in from the fields fatigued and famished. Jacob was preparing soup. Esau said, "Feed me, I pray thee, with that same red pottage; for I am faint." Here the Bible says, "Therefore was his name called Edom" (Genesis 25:29-34). "Edom" means "red." The soup Jacob was preparing was red, possibly red lentils.

Esau moved to "the land of Seir, the country of Edom" (Genesis 32:3; 33:16; 36:8). This is a large section of land in modern-day Jordan, south of the Dead Sea, primarily a range of rugged, high mountains punctuated by steep, awe-inspiring ravines. Petra is within its boundaries.

The Bible calls Esau the "father of the Edomites in Mount Seir" (Genesis 36:9). The Lord said that He gave "mount Seir unto Esau for a possession" (Deuteronomy 2:5). Interestingly, the soil of the land where Esau settled is reddish-brown. So, from start to finish, Esau's life aptly matched his alternate name of "Edom."

On a summit above Petra's ruins is Umm al-Biyara, which means "Mother of all Cisterns." Among the ruins was found a clay seal impression inscribed with the name "Qos-Gabr, King of Edom." Although archaeologists cannot agree as to the date of the seal impression (some suggest the seventh century B.C.), it is testimony that this was indeed an Edomite settlement. Although Esau may not have lived here, Umm al-Biyara was almost certainly home to members of his tribe, the Edomites.

OUR JOURNEY THROUGH EDOM

The day we headed to Petra, we left behind the plush Dead Sea Mövenpick Resort and drove south on Highway 65. Somewhere soon after we passed the Salt Plains, we entered the biblical land of Edom. (The Zered River was the boundary between Edom to the South and Moab to the North, but we did not see it.) We turned east unto unmarked Highway 60.

We came to Tafileh, a town built on the ruins of biblical Tophel (Deuteronomy 1:1). We then turned south on Highway 35. This highway closely follows Jordan's stretch of what for thousands of years has been known as the Kings Highway. It was a trade route that passed through Petra, Karak, Madaba, Amman, and Jerash. It originated in Egypt and ended in a town deep within Syria called Resafa.

Moses asked the Edomites if the children of Israel could use this part of the King's Highway that passed through their land. They refused, and the children of Israel were forced to take a more circuitous and difficult route (Numbers 20:14-21; Judges 11:16-18).

Ah, if these ancient roads could speak, what stories they would tell!

Shortly after our turn onto Highway 35, the little Ford car climbed and climbed, up and down, before it finally protested. We stopped on the top of a hill to let it cool down. There we were, far from a service station, and the few people who drove by us did not stop to ask us if we needed help. (That may have been a good thing.) My mom was with us, but fortunately, neither she nor I get easily alarmed about things like that. We just walked around a little, stretching our legs and enjoying the view of the rocks. After quite a while, Bill filled the radiator with some of our precious drinking water and determined that the car was good to go.

We passed through Buseirah, which is the modern city built near ruins of biblical Bozrah, said to be the capital of the Edomite kingdom. Now we were in the heart of Edom. Bozrah means "sheep fold." It is mentioned throughout Scripture (Genesis 36:33; I Chronicles 1:44; Isaiah 63:1; Amos 1:12; Micah 2:12).

Soon, visibility decreased, and it began to rain a little. Whether we were in fog or clouds, I do not know. Finally, we arrived at a town called Wadi Musa – the Valley of Moses – and checked into Beit Zaman, our hotel-home for two nights while we explored Petra.

Without a doubt, the Edomites of old were a lot tougher than us; we were tired from just one afternoon's drive through Edom in a modern automobile. What it must have been like to live in such a rugged world!

BROTHERS, ENEMIES

Jacob and Esau were twin brothers. Jacob is the ancestor of the Israelites. Esau is the ancestor of the Edomites. To the Israelites, God said, "Thou shalt not abhor an Edomite; for he is thy brother" (Deuteronomy 23:7).

Yet, conflicts seemed inevitable between the two neighboring nations. The saddest part of the conflicts was that, when the Israelites and Edomites fought one another, they were destroying their own blood relatives.

Many of Israel and Judah's kings warred with Edom: Saul (I Samuel 14:47), David (II Samuel 8:14; I Chronicles 18:13; Psalm 60:8-9), Joram (II Kings 8:20-22), Amaziah (II Kings 14:1,7), and Ahaz (II Chronicles 28:16-17).

DOEG

Personally, I think that the story recorded in I Samuel 21-22 is the most heart wrenching of all of the Israelite-Edomite conflicts.

David was fleeing from King Saul and went to the house of the Lord. Ahimelech the priest helped David, giving him food and the sword of Goliath for a weapon.

Almost as a footnote, I Samuel 21:7 tells us that "Doeg, an Edomite, the chiefest of the herdmen that belonged to Saul" was in the temple that day.

Later, Doeg told King Saul that Ahimelech had helped David. In his wrath, King Saul commanded the death of Ahimelech and other priests. "But the servants of the king would not put forth their hand to fall upon the priests of the LORD" (I Samuel 22:17). They had too much reverence for God and His priestly servants.

But King Saul knew who would do his dirty work: Doeg the Edomite. Doeg promptly "slew on that day fourscore and five [85] persons that did wear a linen ephod." His murders continued in "Nob, the city of the priests," with the killing of more men, women, children, babies, and animals (I Samuel 22:18-19).

Why Doeg was living in Israel in the first place, especially in such close alliance with King Saul, is itself a mystery. But what gave him the cold nerve to kill the priests of the Lord, when no one else would? The probable reason why he had no compunction about destroying priests was because Edomites were not true worshippers of Yahweh.

One of Ahimelech's sons, Abiathar, escaped the slaughter, and came to David. From an anguished heart, David lamented, "I have occasioned the death of all the persons of thy father's house" (I Samuel 22:22).

In Psalm 52, David speaks of Doeg. "Thy tongue deviseth mischiefs; like a sharp razor, working deceitfully. Thou lovest evil more than good; and lying rather than to speak righteousness. Lo, this is the man that made not God his strength. But I am like a green olive tree in the house of God: I trust in the mercy of God for ever and ever."

David could have said to Doeg, "Yes, you are my blood relative. But in the ways that matter most – worship and reverence of the One True God – we are not related."

EDOM'S IDOLATRY

Although the Edomites initially had a knowledge of Yahweh, they eventually began to worship multiple gods, especially fertility gods. Their primary god was called Qos.

Because Solomon loved strange women, including Edomite women, his heart was eventually turned away from God. He built high places so his foreign wives could sacrifice to their gods (I Kings 11:1-8).

After King Amaziah had a great victory over the Edomites, "he brought the gods of the children of Seir, and set them up to be his gods, and bowed down himself before them, and burned incense unto them" (II Chronicles 25:14-20).

ESAU'S LEGACY

The Edomites have a sad beginning and a sad ending. Esau will always be known as the brother who despised his birthright (Genesis 25:34). He was the firstborn, and according to Exodus 34:19, the firstborn belonged to the Lord. The firstborn was entrusted with both great blessings and great responsibility, in spiritual and practical matters. For whatever reason, Esau despised his birthright.

So the blessing that should have been his was given to his brother Jacob, who, for all his faults, craved the blessings and benefits of the birthright. Although Esau begged his dying father Isaac to bless him also, the blessing he received was not the one he wanted (Genesis 27:18-40).

Esau failed to value what was most important. Unfortunately, his maverick ways transmitted to generation after generation of Edomites. The Prophets issued scathing denunciations of Edom. The book of Obadiah is devoted completely to the Edomites, replete with language that seems to paint a picture of Petra: "The pride of thine heart hath deceived thee, thou that dwellest in the clefts of the rock, whose habitation is high; that saith in his heart, Who shall bring me down to the ground? Though thou exalt thyself as the eagle, and though thou set thy nest among the stars, thence will I bring thee down, saith the LORD" (Obadiah 1:3-4).

Esau provides us with an intensely sobering lesson. Our single actions – good or evil – can have long-reaching results. We should not underestimate how our priorities will affect our families, friends, and our society. In the Old Testament, God wanted the firstborn to be sanctified to Him, dedicated to Him and Him alone.

Today, God wants the best we have to give Him. He does not want our leftovers. He wants to be first in our lives because He knows that nothing but His Spirit can give us the deep, deep peace we need and crave. If we exalt anything in our hearts above Him, then that is what we worship and that is what we trust.

PAUL AND PETRA

In II Corinthians 11:32-33, Paul recounts that "In Damascus the governor under Aretas the king kept the city of the Damascenes with a garrison, desirous to apprehend me: And through a window in a basket was I let down by the wall, and escaped his hands."

Acts 9:1-27 provides more background and details to Paul's account in II Corinthians. Damascus, Syria is the setting of Paul's dramatic conversion experience. There Paul's physical and spiritual eyesight were restored. He was filled with the Holy Ghost and baptized. He did not immediately return to Jerusalem but he stayed "certain days with the disciples which were at Damascus."

The gospel is powerful, and overnight Paul went from being a persecutor of the gospel to an evangelist promoting the gospel. He went into the synagogues, places where Jews gathered to worship and learn, and "preached Christ."

Not everyone was thrilled about Paul's conversion, even though it meant that he was no longer trying to imprison and punish innocent people. Soon after, "the Jews took counsel to kill him." People were assigned to lay in wait for Paul, to apprehend him. But "the disciples took him by night, and let him down by the wall in a basket" and he escaped.

This account is similar to how Rahab helped Joshua's two spies escape from Jericho. "Then she let them down by a cord through the window: for her house was upon the town wall, and she dwelt upon the wall" (Joshua 2:15). In Bible days, domestic dwellings were built along the rock walls of the city. Small openings, or windows, made it possible for such escapes.

Aretas IV was the king of the Nabatean kingdom of Petra and the surrounding area. An article in the Jewish Encyclopedia says this about Aretas IV: "Being the most powerful neighbor of Judea, he frequently took part in the state affairs of that country, and was influential in shaping the destiny of its rulers."[1] Aretas IV was father-in-law to Herod Antipas. It is likely that Aretas IV may have favored this marriage to encourage political harmony with Israel and Rome.

Damascus was under the control of Aretas IV. Apparently, the Jews appealed to the ruling government leaders to assist them in apprehending Paul. Exactly how much involvement Aretas IV had in this plan is unknown, for Scripture and history are silent on the subject.

But it is probable that the governor who worked under the authority of Aretas IV was in favor of suppressing Paul's voice as he spoke of Jesus in Jewish synagogues. It is quite likely that Aretas IV, an idolatrous king, would not have been in favor of Paul's message.

PETRA: PAST, PRESENT, AND FUTURE

Petra is one of the New Seven Wonders of the World. Its eclectic blend of architectural styles, combined with the sheer wonder of its creation, make Petra an amazing and unforgettable place to visit.

In 1993, King Hussein of Jordan said, "Petra is a stunning physical monument from ancient times, but it is also much more than that; it is a timeless message that speaks to us still of an eternal human capacity to dare, and therefore to achieve bold feats and beautiful wonders."[2]

John William Burgon, a British theologian, is remembered by history as a fierce opponent to Westcott and Hort, the two men chiefly responsible for the revision of the King James Version of the Bible.

But Burgon also went down in history for his poem simply entitled *Petra*. Though he never visited Petra, he formulated his poem from explorers' descriptions. The poem's famous line describes Petra as "A rose-red city – 'half as old as time.'"

Petra's past connections to the land of Israel – from the Edomites to the Nabateans – have definite and important biblical links. Today, Petra serves simply as a tourist attraction. Even the Bedouins that once lived in some of Petra's many caves have been relocated to nearby desert housing.

But some people believe that Petra is only lying dormant, until it is once again inhabited. It is possible that Petra might be where the Jews will flee during a time of future tribulation. Prophecy students point to verses such as Isaiah 33:16, Micah 2:12-13 and Matthew 24:16 to support their supposition.

Prophecy is one topic I have little interest in, so I am highly unqualified to comment on this idea. But I do know that Petra is a natural stronghold, an excellent defensive position. If I needed to suddenly escape from Jerusalem, I might head to Petra. As the crow flies, the two cities are only about 100 miles apart.

Regardless of what the future holds for Petra, its past holds many lessons for us today. We simply need to consider the records of men such as Esau and Doeg, King Solomon and King Amaziah. Unfortunately, it is their mistakes that provide our lesson material.

But, if we take heed to their errors, we can walk a different path than they chose. Past the din of tourists' voices and camels' bellows, Petra's rose-red walls echo a message: "Learn, glean...remember."

Tip for the Traveler

If you visit Petra in the summer, make sure you wear a hat, sunglasses, and sunscreen. Keep water with you at all times. The desert sun gives "hot" a new definition and if you are not used to the weather, you can become dehydrated without realizing it.

For a price, you can ride in a horse-drawn cart, or on the back of a camel or donkey. Be prepared to dicker a little on the price, unless you prefer to pay top dollar for your ride.

The best time to take photographs of Petra is in the late afternoon hours, just before sunset, as the colors of the rocks soften in the fading light.

Martha's Dilemma

Luke 10:38-42

"Now it came to pass, as they went, that he entered into a
certain village: and a certain woman named Martha received
him into her house. And she had a sister called Mary, which
also sat at Jesus' feet, and heard his word.

But Martha was cumbered about much serving, and came to
him, and said, Lord, dost thou not care that my sister hath left
me to serve alone? bid her therefore that she help me.

And Jesus answered and said unto her, Martha, Martha, thou
art careful and troubled about many things: But one thing is
needful: and Mary hath chosen that good part, which shall not
be taken away from her."

When the story of Mary and Martha is discussed,
Martha often gets slightly berated for her failure to sit at Jesus'
feet. It is tempting to simplistically conclude that Mary was
spiritual and Martha was carnal. While Mary wanted to listen to
Jesus, Martha was more interested in doing.

Mary gets the star and Martha has to sit in the corner
of the room. We figure that it is better to pray than cook for

the potluck supper, and spiritual things always trump natural things. While there certainly is truth in this, there is a much deeper dynamic and lesson here that few people realize.

Beyond the simple spiritual-versus-carnal lesson, I think Jesus was trying to teach two less obvious principles that we can apply to many areas of our lives: 1) Sometimes it is needful to break free from cultural norms and 2) Misplaced priorities can be detrimental.

According to cultural norms, Martha was doing exactly what was proper: She was serving her guests. To do otherwise would have been a terrible slight to visitors. In Martha's society, failure to prepare food and drink for guests was unthinkable. Her womanhood was defined in great part by her ability to serve her family and guests.

During our tenure in Jordan, we spent a lot of time in people's homes. I do not remember one instance of being in a home where we were not served food (usually fruit or cookies) and drink (usually tea or juice). Many people in Jordan do not have a lot of material possessions but they are generous with what they do have. Middle Eastern women are such gracious hostesses that I feel quite clumsy by comparison.

When Martha asked Jesus to tell Mary to help her, she was appealing to their society's inbred understanding of a woman's place in their culture. Their proper role in society dictated that women take care of the home and children. Today, in Jordan, few women work outside their homes. Even if you walk into a women's clothing store, nine times out of ten you will find a man serving as the clerk, not a woman. Although a few women work in grocery stores and hospitals, it is understood that these are exceptions to the norm.

Then as now, as a traditional woman living in the Middle East, it was unacceptable to mix with men. Many of the homes we visited were guided by this rule. To a great extent, men fellowship with men and women fellowship with women, sometimes even in separate rooms.

When Mary opted to sit at Jesus' feet instead of helping Martha in the kitchen, she became a woman in a man's world. By entering a room full of men, as though she was one of them, she removed herself from her proper role in society. So, although we understand that we should be more like Mary and less like Martha, there is more here than at first meets the eye.

Jesus was trying to help people understand that sometimes the gospel contradicts culture. And when it does, we must follow the gospel. In this case, although what Martha was doing was entirely right, regarding the role of women, there was a higher law at work here. Mary discovered that "good part." She somehow realized that her acceptable role could be set aside for a higher way of life. While Mary instinctively understood this, Martha had to be taught it.

Jesus invited "whosoever will" to follow Him (Mark 8:34). Anyone and everyone – male or female, Jew or Gentile, poor or rich – was welcome. Jesus did not validate the barriers in His society. In fact, during His ministry, Jesus was constantly uprooting traditions and unseating cultural norms. He fought against deeply rooted mindsets. Some of the mindsets, in and of themselves, were not necessarily evil. But when they caused people to be stuck in a rut, Jesus presented a superior alternative.

When Jesus told Martha, "You are careful and troubled about many things," He was letting her know that her problem was her loyalty to cultural norms when something more important was occurring. She was worried about what people might think about her if she went against the status quo. Although she was doing what was right and proper, she failed to recognize that God was trying to work in her life. Note that nowhere in the passage did Jesus actually condemn Martha for her hospitality and service. He only pointed out her misplaced priority, which was causing her to be agitated and upset. It is okay to serve as long as our deeds are motivated by pure love for Jesus and our focus is on Him.

We can learn a lot from this passage. Sometimes we feel compelled to mirror the customs and mindsets of our society. Driven by fear of rejection, we feel pressured to conform. As our world gyrates with change, from modesty limits in clothing styles to the acceptance of once shunned sins, we are bombarded with pressure to follow their trends.

Because we are Americans, we do American things and we think like Americans. We never pause to consider that our loyalty to American culture should be far exceeded by loyalty to our King who rules a nation far superior to America or any other earthly country.

Some things about America are not necessarily evil but our adherence to them can inadvertently cause us to have misplaced priorities. For example, America was built on principles of hard work, entrepreneurship, and solidarity. These are some of the concepts that made America great. Here, you could become almost anything you wanted to become. Dreams could become reality.

Whereas these principles are not evil in and of themselves, for some they can become detrimental. A man can choose to be a workaholic and neglect his family, creating insecurity and resentment among them. An entrepreneur can become so focused on making his business successful that he fails to spend time in prayer and misses church services to work late, eventually becoming spiritually lukewarm.

We must be committed to keeping the Kingdom of God in sharp focus. It will not happen automatically. In the Old Testament, God warned His people against assimilation (Leviticus 18:26-27; Deuteronomy 12:29-31; 18:9). You will live among them but do not worship their gods, He said. Do not follow their customs. Blending is never acceptable.

When we try to fit in with the world around us, we are attempting the impossible. We are simply not one of them. We are peculiar, or special, people (Titus 2:14). We are a holy, or separate, nation that has been called out of darkness (I Peter 2:9). We might be Americans, but we are also citizens of a greater nation.

When choices have to be made, our loyalty to our heavenly home should surpass loyalty to our earthly home. Sometimes we will have to completely abandon certain activities and concepts. With other things, we will just have to keep first things first. Just as it was not wrong for Martha to serve, so some things will not be wrong for us to do, as long as our priorities and motives are right.

Mary was misunderstood by her sister Martha. When we go against the status quo and break free from cultural norms, we should expect to be misunderstood, even ridiculed at times. Until onlookers break free from the kitchen and enter the presence of Jesus, they simply will not understand the beauty of things they find so repulsive.

Just as Jesus admonished Martha to readjust her priorities and lay aside her innate habits that were so comfortable to her, He sometimes asks us to do the same. When we must make a choice, our guiding charter must be the Bible, its examples, and the principles of the Kingdom of God. It is a higher law, a superior way of life.

Tip for the Traveler

If you are ever invited into a Middle Eastern home, chances are good that you will be the beneficiary of some delightful hospitality. If the home is poor, keep in mind that you are probably being served the best food they have, so always be a gracious guest.

Usually you will be offered coffee. Bill and I do not drink coffee, so hosts accommodate us with hot tea or juice instead. If you are a coffee drinker, be warned: Middle Eastern coffee is really strong, so be prepared for a jolt! If you have had enough coffee, shake your cup sideways. Until you do so, you cup will be refilled as soon as you empty it.

One cultural tip: Do not sit in such a way that the bottom of your foot is lifted in the direction of your host or other guests. Since many Middle Easterners consider feet and shoes unclean, this is considered a terrible insult. So be sure to not sit with your legs crossed; keep your feet flat on the floor.

With all this said, being in a Middle Easterner's home will bring the warm hospitality of the Bible to life, so enjoy...and try to keep your coffee intake to a minimum!

Encounter at the Ford Jabbok

Today it is a polluted stream, littered with debris. Here and there discarded tires unpleasantly adorn the riverbank. Jordanians call the river by its modern name, the Zarqa, which is Arabic for "Blue." The Bible calls it the Jabbok. It is one of the two main tributaries of the Jordan River. (The other tributary is the Yarmouk River.)

From a distance the Zarqa River is picturesque, flowing gently between lush hillsides. But years of ingesting industrial waste, chemicals, and raw sewage have taken their toll on this important waterway. Although the water is used for irrigation purposes, it is unsafe to drink. The Kingdom of Jordan is taking steps to purify the river, but the process of decontamination will take time.

Once a week, on our way to Bible studies in northern Jordan, the road we traveled descended into a deep valley. Here, we crossed over the Zarqa River by way of a modern bridge. But thousands of years ago another stranger, without the convenience of a bridge, crossed this river too. Jacob, that troubled, torn man, who deceived others and was in turn deceived *by* others, had to make a transition. That transition was a pivotal point in his life and it occurred on the banks of this river.

Only twice did we have time to stop and walk down to the riverbank. Once, a group of Muslim women were sitting side by side, relaxing by the river. Apparently, none of them spoke much English and our Arabic was sparse, so we used sign language. One of the ladies put her hand in mine and wanted her picture taken with me. Her friend used her cell phone to snap the shot. I took the action as either a sign of hospitable camaraderie or excitement at meeting an American.

Thousands of years ago, Jacob had an encounter at the Zarqa River, which he called the Jabbok. But his encounter was entirely different from mine. Rather than grasping the hand of a human being in a friendly gesture, he wrestled with a divine being. My meeting with those ladies was casual and insignificant. Jacob's meeting changed the course of his life.

Throughout history, rivers have often been remembered for their association with great battles. Two examples from America's history are the Battle of Bull Run and the Battle of the Little Bighorn. The Battle of Bull Run was the first major military conflict of the United States' Civil War. It was called the Battle of Bull Run because of its proximity to the Bull Run stream in Virginia. The Battle of the Little Bighorn is also known as Custer's Last Stand. On the plains of the Little Bighorn River in Montana, Lieutenant Colonel Custer met his death and the Americans suffered a brutal defeat at the hands of Indian forces.

From birth, some people seem to have the odds against them. As Jacob was being born, he caught the heel of his older twin brother, Esau. Because of this action, he was named "Jacob." This name meant "Heel-catcher, Supplanter, Deceiver." In Bible days, a name was an integral part of who a person was. Jacob's destiny seemed sealed from the moment he took his first breath. He grew up parented by a mother and father who played favorites. His mother, Rebekah, loved Jacob but his father, Isaac, loved Esau (Genesis 25:28). His family was rife with dysfunction.

Jacob grew up with a label on his life, a label that he did not choose, but one that he was powerless to remove. Each time someone called his name, he was reminded of who he was. Jacob…Deceiver. It was seared into his mind, infused into his very being.

Esau, as the elder brother, was entitled to the birthright. He despised it, however, perhaps because of the responsibility it represented. Jacob, on the other hand, wanted the birthright. With only a little persuasion, Esau sold it to him for a bowl of lentils.

Years passed, and it was time for Isaac to die. He told Esau to go hunting and prepare meat for him to eat. He would then bless Esau, the firstborn. When Esau left, Rebekah told Jacob to deceive Isaac and obtain the blessing.

At first, Jacob resisted his mother's scheme. He did not want his father to think he was a deceiver. He was unwilling to admit that Isaac had been calling Jacob a deceiver all his life. He craved his father's approval. He wanted to be called something good, something other than "Heel-Catcher, Supplanter, Deceiver." But finally Jacob's mother convinced him to follow through with her plan.

So Jacob obtained the blessing and had scarcely left Isaac's bedside when Esau returned. When Esau discovered what Jacob had done, "he cried with a great and exceeding bitter cry" (Genesis 27:34). Although Isaac issued a blessing to Esau also, it was a blessing laced with bitterness. Esau was destined to live by the sword and be in subjection to his younger brother Jacob.

The Bible says that "Esau hated Jacob because of the blessing wherewith his father blessed him" (Geneses 27:41.) He purposed to kill Jacob as soon as Isaac was dead. To save her son's life, Rebekah devised another scheme. She convinced Isaac that Jacob needed to go to Padan-aram, also called Haran. This was in northern modern-day Syria, about 550 miles from Beersheba, Jacob's home.

Esau had married Canaanite women and they were a "grief of mind" to Isaac and Rebekah. So Rebekah had no trouble convincing Isaac to send Jacob to a place where he could marry a woman from their own tribe. This guise successfully saved Jacob from being subjected to the force of Esau's wrath.

Jacob left all that was familiar to him to begin a new life. Along his journey, at Bethel, God affirmed to Jacob the promise that He had made to Jacob's grandfather Abraham. In turn, Jacob vowed to God, " If God will be with me, and will keep me in this way that I go, and will give me bread to eat, and raiment to put on, So that I come again to my father's house in peace; then shall the Lord be my God" (Genesis 28:20-21). This reveals what was probably Jacob's greatest desire: Peace in his family.

During his twenty-year sojourn in Padan-aram, Jacob married Leah and Rachel, sisters. They and their handmaids bore him eleven sons. Jacob became a prosperous and wealthy man. But the prosperity came at a painful cost: Jacob and his father-in-law Laban deceived each other to get what they both wanted. It seems that Jacob's cycle was continuing: he was both deceiving and being deceived.

In time, God began to make the nest uncomfortable for Jacob. Laban was upset with Jacob and a serious family conflict seemed imminent. At this point, the Lord told Jacob that it was time to go home.

Jacob had one chief concern: his brother Esau. Esau lived in Edom, in southern modern-day Jordan. To try to appease Esau's anger, Jacob sent him gifts of animals and servants. But Esau was not deterred. Jacob's messengers told him that Esau was coming to meet him with four hundred seasoned warriors. Jacob stood to lose not just all he had gained during the last twenty years, but his life as well. He "was greatly afraid and distressed" (Genesis 32:7).

That momentous night, Jacob came to the Ford Jabbok. A ford is a low spot in a river that can serve as a place to easily cross the river. Jacob sent his family and possessions across this ford in the Jabbok River, which was near Peniel, but he lingered behind them...alone.

Jacob had reached the end of himself. There, as the water flowed past, he realized that he was at a dead-end street with no one to help him except God. He had exhausted his resources and his plans had failed. Esau was not deterred; he wanted revenge. Family peace seemed an impossible dream.

Suddenly, a Man appeared. And He began to wrestle with Jacob. All night they wrestled, not so much for physical pre-eminence, but as a reflection of the struggle in Jacob's heart. There on the banks of that river, Jacob was facing the worst battle of his life. In Hebrew, Jabbok (Yabboq) has its root in "baqaq," which means "to pour out, to empty." Jacob's meeting with this divine being was a time of confrontation, awareness, honesty...desperation.

Then, as dawn broke, the Man asked Jacob to tell Him his name. Such a strange question. Why ask a person his name? Because Jacob's name identified him for who he really was.

No doubt from the anguish of the depths of his being, he said, "Jacob. My name is Deceiver." Perhaps this was one of the most difficult things Jacob ever did. God wanted Jacob to admit who he was. Jacob had been wrestling all of his life with the label that had been his from birth. It was time for a change.

Jacob, I am going to give you a new name. You will have a new identity. From this day forward, your name will be Israel, "for as a prince hast thou power with God and with men, and hast prevailed" (Genesis 32:28). Jacob's encounter at the Ford Jabbok was a turning point in his life. Not only did God mend Jacob's relationship with his brother Esau, but He equipped Jacob with a relationship with Him that he had never before had.

That lonely river was the site of an intense personal struggle, the result of which forever altered Jacob's identity. He was never the same.

Jacob called the location of his encounter Peniel, which means "the face of God." He said, "I have seen God face to face, and my life is preserved" (Genesis 32:30). Jacob had an encounter with God...and a person who encounters God will be forever changed.

Ben Yehuda and Hebrew

Just one short block from our apartment in Jerusalem is Ben Yehuda Street, Jerusalem's lively pedestrian mall. Here you can purchase anything from Cuban cigars to flowers to Judaic gifts. At night, the street becomes even livelier, as people come out of the woodwork and street musicians set up camp.

A harpist frequents the plaza with her lovely music. Further down the street you might hear drums or a clarinet. A small group of young people may gather to sing a cappella. At the end of the street is Zion Square, a site that hosts political demonstrations from time to time. It is not uncommon to see a group of Haredi men plying pamphlets across the street from dreadlock-wearing hippies making a statement by strumming box guitars and singing American songs from the '60s.

In many ways, Ben Yehuda Street is much more than a tourist trap. It is the modern expression of youthful hope and activity. The intersecting roads and alleys beckon pedestrians to explore them. Bounded on one end by Jaffa Street and the other by King George Street, the Ben Yehuda Street neighborhood is a tidy rectangle of bustling activity, where friends meet for a French crepe or an elegant dinner.

Since I am really a city girl at heart, I find it fun to step out of our apartment building each day, walk a few steps onto Ben Yehuda Street, and go from there to our destinations. At night, voices and horns blend with the sounds of feral cats and nightclubs, creating quite an interesting backdrop as we close our days.

When we first arrived in Jerusalem, we were told about a Hebrew language class. Unfortunately, the level of most of the students was far beyond ours, so we did not continue the lessons.

But the elderly instructor told us something interesting. At some point in her life, she had lived with Eliezer Ben Yehuda's daughter for a while. The two of them studied Arabic together.

I had read a biography of Eliezer Ben Yehuda and became mildly fascinated with his life. He was born in Lithuania as Eliezer Titzhak Perelman. His parents were Hassidic Jews, but eventually Ben Yehuda became less religious and more politically attuned, especially in regards to Zionism. He changed his name to the more Hebrew-sounding Eliezer Ben Yehuda.

Ben Yehuda is the father of the modern Hebrew language. Throughout the years, Hebrew had fallen out of use. Because Jews had been dispersed throughout the world for almost 2,000 years, many of them had adopted the language of the country where they lived, whether it was Germany, Russia, Romania or some other place. Most of them did not speak Hebrew at all.

In the late 1800s and early 1900s, Zionists became more aggressive and Jews began returning to the land of Israel.

Ben Yehuda knew that a united language was necessary to bond the people. He devoted his entire life to reviving this language and writing a dictionary.

Ben Yehuda was opposed and persecuted by many people, even Jews, who at the time could not envision the necessity of a common language among them. He persevered, despite battling tuberculosis and bearing the grief of the deaths of his wife and several children. He was persecuted by Haredi Jews who believed that he was profaning the sacred by making Hebrew a language for common use.

Yiddish is a German-based language spoken by Ashkenazi Jews since the 10th century. It was highly influenced by other languages besides German, including Hebrew, Aramaic, and Eastern European languages. These days, it is primarily spoken by Haredi Jews. Ben Yehuda rejected Yiddish because he considered it a corrupted language.

Ben Yehuda Street is named for Eliezer Ben Yehuda. The man who endured poverty, ridicule, and rejection is now celebrated for contributing to the modern nation of Israel's success, where Hebrew is one of the official languages. (Arabic is the other.)

But in a strange twist of irony, through the years since Israel's inception in 1948, Ben Yehuda Street has become a preferred location for terrorist bombings.

One day, as Bill and I were working in the school office, we heard someone outside speaking Hebrew over a loudspeaker. We did not pay much attention to it, since our neighborhood is noisy, and we did not understand Hebrew very well anyway. But a few minutes later, we heard it again so I stepped out onto the small balcony to see what was going on.

A police van was parked on Ben Yehuda Street, with a ramp lowered. As I watched, a robot came down the ramp onto the street. It was black and bulky, about the length of a motorcycle. It went down Ben Yehuda Street to "sniff" for bombs. Thankfully, the coast was clear.

The next day, however, we heard a bomb explode near the central bus station, about a mile away from our apartment. Bus #74 was hit, about 20 people were injured, and one woman died. The bombing was a sober reminder to us to always be aware and cautious, especially when walking down Ben Yehuda Street and when in other congested areas.

Eliezer means "God helps" and Ben Yehuda means "Son of Judah" or "Son of Praise." Truly, God did help Ben Yehuda and used his life to provide a unifying language for modern Jews.

When Ben Yehuda died, finally succumbing to tuberculosis at the age of 64, 30,000 people came to his funeral over a three-day mourning span. Before His death, the last word Ben Yehuda restored was "nefesh," which means "soul."

This word is used many times throughout the Bible. One of the first mentions is Genesis 2:7, which reads, "And the LORD God formed man of the dust of the ground, and breathed into his nostrils the breath of life; and man became a living soul."

It seems fitting that "nefesh" was Ben Yehuda's final word to study. God is truly the One who gives and takes the breath of life. He alone is the Source of life eternal. "Nefesh" is a reminder to us of our frailty when contrasted to God's greatness and power.

Zephaniah 3:8 is the only verse in the Old Testament that uses all 22 letters of the Hebrew alphabet.[1] The very next verse says, "For then will I turn to the people a pure language, that they may all call upon the name of the LORD, to serve him with one consent." The placement of these verses hardly seems coincidental.

I find it interesting that "pure" in this prophetic passage translates to mean "to examine, to cleanse, to choose, to polish." This is what Ben Yehuda did. Though modern Hebrew differs from biblical Hebrew, Hebrew is once again the language of the land of Israel, the tongue by which "they may all call upon the name of the LORD, to serve him with one consent."

Tip for the Traveler

The Ben Yehuda Street neighborhood is a great place to eat and shop. There is a variety of restaurants, cafes and bakeries. Here you can get everything from McDonalds to falafels. Several non-Kosher restaurants are open on Shabbat, the day when most shops and businesses are closed. (Shabbat begins at sundown Friday and ends at sundown Saturday.)

Some of the small shops have a lovely selection of modest clothing at reasonable prices. Often, the garments are not marked with prices. If this is the case, do not be afraid to offer shopkeepers less than the price they quote. In many shops, this is an acceptable practice.

Also, the intersection of Ben Yehuda Street and King George Street is a great place to catch a bus or taxi. Since we operate on a fixed budget, we use the buses, but most visitors opt to use taxis for purposes of security and convenience. Buses are much cheaper than taxis, but it does take more time to get to a destination since buses have to follow scheduled routes. If you are traveling on your own and plan to use taxis a lot, factor adequate transportation fees into your budget.

The Blight of Barrenness

Bill and I have been married since 1993. We never anticipated that we would not have children. We both wanted children, but they never came along. From time to time, that maternal instinct tugs at my heart. Occasionally, when Bill and I are around children and young people, we talk later about how nice it would be if we had some of our own children to love, train, and nurture.

In American society it is acceptable to be childless. And it is possible to live a fulfilling life without children. We have prayed many times for God to have His will in our lives. We do not want to push open a door that God has closed. So, at some point long ago, we subconsciously settled into a place of acceptance. We are content with life as it is, just the two of us.

God told the first couple – Adam and Eve – to be fruitful and multiply (Genesis 1:28). Jesus loved to have children around Him (Matthew 19:14). I like the word picture of Psalm 128:3: "Thy wife shall be as a fruitful vine by the sides of thine house: thy children like olive plants round about thy table." Psalm 127:4-5 is also picturesque: "As arrows are in the hand of a mighty man; so are children of the youth. Happy is the man that hath his quiver full of them." It is obvious from Scripture that bearing and raising children is God's plan.

In Bible times, deviation from this plan was the exception, not the norm.

Yet, occasionally God must have other plans. Though we do not understand His ways, we have learned to rest in His knowledge and wisdom. And since America is in the process of redefining the term "family" and altering God's original design for marriage and family, a childless couple experiences little societal pressure. In America, life without children is not considered unusual.

But it is not so everywhere. Living childless in the Middle East is an educational experience. I am often asked how many children I have. When I tell people I do not have any children, they think something is wrong with me. I once told an elderly Arab woman that I was content with my life; she looked at me like I was crazy. I do not remember meeting even one Middle Eastern married woman without children.

Why is childbearing so important in the Middle East? Because that culture, which is vastly different from Western culture, follows the model of thousands of years of tradition. In their society, a woman's worth is determined largely by her ability to marry and birth children. Thus, if a woman is barren, her worth is compromised.

In Jordan, if a child is not conceived after six months of marriage, the wife must go to a doctor to see what can be done to help her conceive. Fertility clinics are easy to find, because they serve to address a key issue in society.

Grandparents will pressure their children to give them grandchildren. Family lineage is very important. It is shameful to not provide your husband with children to carry on the family name. So boys especially are anticipated. I know one family with three daughters. They are lovely girls, but because the wife did not bear a son, it has created problems in the marriage.

In both the traditional Jewish and Arab worlds, barrenness is a terrible state to find oneself. Why a woman would be unmarried or married without children is unfathomable to the minds of many Middle Easterners.

This is reminiscent of biblical times. In addition to the pain of not being able to fulfill instinctual maternal longings, a barren woman endured ridicule for her shameful, childless condition. She lived, day in and day out, with a stigma. She could not provide a male heir for her husband, a man to continue the family name.

I find it fascinating that the patriarchs of the Bible – Abram, Isaac, and Jacob – all had barren wives.

When Sarai, Abram's wife, could not conceive a child, she resorted to an acceptable custom of her time. She offered her handmaid Hagar to her husband. The custom dictated that a barren wife could adopt the child birthed by the handmaid and the child could become a legal heir.

(Later, God told Abram to cast out Hagar and her son Ishmael. According to God, only the child of promise, Isaac, was legitimately entitled to inherit and enter a covenant relationship with Him. In the New Testament, the child of the bondwoman (Hagar) was used to symbolize the product of the flesh, or the will of man. The child of the freewoman (Sarai) symbolized the product of the promise of God. See Genesis 17:19; 21:10-13; Galatians 4:23-31. God and Abram had a similar conversation about Eliezer. See Genesis 15:1-4.)

Human nature being what it is, this custom was not ideal and was not void of jealousy and resentment between the two women. Once Sarai had her true birth child (Isaac) in her arms, she no longer wanted the surrogate child (Ishmael). In the end, Sarai's attempt to control circumstances backfired on her. Rather than wait on God to fulfill His promise, she chose a human, almost businesslike arrangement, to achieve the goal.

It is hard to fault Sarai, since she had no Bible to read. She was one of the Bible's first leading ladies. She was a pioneer and had no previous stories about miraculous births to bolster her faith. All she could see was the shame of her barrenness.

Listen with your heart to the words of Rachel, Hannah, and Elisabeth. These are three biblical women that lived during different time periods, but they had one thing in common: They bore the shame and reproach of childlessness.

Rachel, Jacob's wife, pleaded with her husband, "Give me children, or else I die." "Jacob's anger was kindled against Rachel: and he said, Am I in God's stead, who hath withheld from thee the fruit of the womb?" Here we see barrenness triggering marital conflict. When Rachel finally bore a son, Joseph, she said, "God hath taken away my reproach" (Genesis 30:1-2,23).

Hannah had a good husband, Elkanah, but no children. Her husband's other wife "provoked her sore, for to make her fret." Elkanah asked her, "Hannah, why weepest thou? and why eatest thou not? and why is thy heart grieved? am not I better to thee than ten sons?" It is apparent that Elkanah loved Hannah and wanted to comfort her in spite of her inability to give him a son.

But Hannah was driven by the shame on her life. With anguish in her soul, she said to the Lord, "If thou wilt indeed look on the affliction of thine handmaid, and remember me, and not forget thine handmaid, but wilt give unto thine handmaid a man child, then I will give him unto the LORD all the days of his life" (I Samuel 1:6,8,11). The Lord heard Hannah's heart's cry, and gave her Samuel, who she then committed to the service of the Lord. Thus, she was released from her shame.

Elisabeth, the mother of John the Baptist, conceived in her old age after many years of barrenness. She said, "Thus hath the Lord dealt with me in the days wherein he looked on me, to take away my reproach among men" (Luke 1:25).

Psalm 113:9 is a beautiful verse which summarizes the role of a woman during Bible days: "He maketh the barren woman to keep house, and to be a joyful mother of children."

Because biblical people would clearly understand the analogy, God often used barrenness to describe the nation of Israel's spiritual condition. If Israel would follow His plan and serve Him, He promised to bless their land with fruitfulness. The women would not be barren or "cast their young" (miscarry). Their land and animals would be fruitful as well (Exodus 23:26; Deuteronomy 7:14; 28:4; Job 21:10; Malachi 3:10-11).

There is a similar principle outlined in the New Testament. As we cultivate the fruit of the Spirit in our lives, we will "neither be barren nor unfruitful in the knowledge of our Lord Jesus Christ" (II Peter 1:5-8).

In the New Testament, the Greek word for "barren" – argos – also translates to mean "idle" and "unemployed."

(Read Matthew 20:1-7). Just as the Israelites had to be pro-active in their obedience and service to God, so we have to be willing to work in the Lord's vineyard. In these New Testament times, it is much more shameful to be spiritually barren than it is to be physically barren.

Keeping in mind the spiritual analogy we can draw for our own lives, a fresh understanding of how biblical people viewed barrenness enables us to better understand their unique challenges. In particular, we can view with greater sympathy and appreciation the women of the Bible whose lives swung the pendulum from bitter barrenness to blessed bountifulness.

Ketef Hinnom

We were in search of Ketef Hinnom, the archaeological burial site where two tiny silver amulets were discovered in 1979. Why was I so interested in these amulets and seeing the place where they were discovered? *Because they are the oldest surviving copies of biblical text.* Dating to the late 7th century B.C., they are about 400 years older than the more renowned Dead Sea Scrolls. The Dead Sea Scrolls were a marvelous find, and in terms of volume, these amulets cannot compare to them.

The amulets are remarkable, not only because they are the oldest copies of biblical text, but because *they contain the oldest inscription of the name of God: YHWH.*

The two amulets are displayed in the Israel Museum in Jerusalem. They are incredibly small, about 1" x 3-3/4" and 1/2" x 1-1/2". They are so thin that I could barely detect the inscriptions, even though the smaller one was positioned behind a magnifying glass. The explanatory sign beside them states: "The amulets, inscribed in the ancient Hebrew script, were found rolled into tiny scrolls in a burial cave in Jerusalem. They were incised with a sharp, thin stylus no thicker than a hair's breadth, and thus deciphering the inscription was difficult."

Scholars were eventually able to discern that the amulets contained the Priestly Benediction, found in Numbers 6:24-26. The Lord told Moses that Aaron and his sons should speak these words to the children of Israel. Even today, rabbis repeat these words every Shabbat in Orthodox synagogues.

On the small amulet was written these words: "[For so-and-so, (the son/daughter of...] h/hu. May h[e]/sh[e] be blessed by YHWH, the warrior and the rebuker of [Evil]: May YHWH bless you, keep you. May YHWH make his face shine upon you and grant you p[ea]ce."

The large amulet was similar and scholars were able to distinguish the following: "[...]YHW...the grea[t...who keeps] the covenant and [g]raciousness toward those who love [him] and those who keep [his commandments...] the Eternal [...] [the?] blessing more than any [sna]re and more than Evil. For redemption is in him. For YHWH is our restorer [and] rock. May YHWH bles[s] you and [may he] keep you. [May] YHWH make [his face] shine..."

Ketef Hinnom means "shoulder of Hinnom." If I remember correctly, modern-day Jews pronounce it "Kay-teff Hee-gnome." It is a hill near Hebron Road that overlooks the Hinnom Valley.

A guide book got us to the general area, but its directions were not precise enough. We walked up Hebron Road, where we saw a sign that said "Bible Hill." I thought that this might be Ketef Hinnom. We climbed up Bible Hill and were rewarded with a beautiful view of Mount Zion and the Old City...but no burial cave. We sat on some concrete blocks, enjoying our view of Jerusalem, joking about the "ancient" concrete structures. We could see St. Andrews Church of Scotland, which the guide book said was next to the cave, but a barbed wire fence kept us from accessing the property from Bible Hill. I later learned that this hill is termed Bible Hill because the tribes of Judah and Benjamin used this ridge to mark their boundaries (Joshua 15:8; 18:16).

We climbed down the hill and finally found the front gate of the Scottish Church. The clerk in the guest house/church knew nothing about the cave. Only when we described to him what it looked like did he remember that this famous cave was on his property! Anyway, we found the cave. What we were able to view was the lower portion of the burial site, since the upper portion was razed years ago during quarrying excavations.

In Bible days, people were generally buried in family tombs, usually cave-type structures that were hewn out of rocks. Multiple generations would use these tombs. A good example of this is Abraham's family. Abraham purchased a cave in Machpelah. The Bible records that Abraham and Sarah, Isaac and Rebekah, and Jacob and Leah were all buried in this same cave (Genesis 23:3-20; 49:29-32).

At Ketef Hinnom, spaces configured to the shape and size of human bodies were carved on the floor of the tomb. We could even detect the outline of the place where the heads would lie. When a family member died, he or she was placed in one of these spaces.

Periodically, the skeletons of the dead would be removed and placed in a pit that was in the middle of the cave. If gifts had been buried with the body, they would be placed in this pit too. Here at Ketef Hinnom, archaeologists discovered pieces of pottery, iron, and alabaster, remnants of long-forgotten but once-treasured gifts. This is where the two silver amulets were found. The process of periodic skeleton transfer freed the spaces for the burial of other bodies. One person I met told me that this procedure was practiced once a year.

So, when the Bible says that a person "slept with his fathers" or was "gathered unto his people," it is referring to the common custom of burying family members in the same tomb. (For examples, read Genesis 35:29; 49:33; I Kings 2:10; II Chronicles 9:31).

Of all the places I visited in Jerusalem, Ketef Hinnom, an almost forgotten site, was to me one of the most significant. Written on tiny, fragile silver fragments, is God's name. He wants us to know Who He is.

I find it incredibly mindboggling that God would allow the oldest biblical manuscript ever found to be such a beautiful expression of His goodness. It is a rich reminder of God's eagerness to bless us, to be our protector and source of peace.

He is not a distant, unconcerned god, but the One True God whose nature is inherently good, generous, and kind. As a gracious father smiles down upon his children, so does our God's face shine upon us.

Numbers 6:24-26

"The LORD bless thee, and keep thee:
The LORD make his face shine upon thee,
and be gracious unto thee:
The LORD lift up his countenance upon thee,
and give thee peace."

Herods of the Bible

When we read the New Testament, it is easy to get confused when we read the word "Herod" because this name belonged to several different people. Sometimes "Herod" refers to Herod the Great. Other times, it refers to one of his sons or grandsons.

For well over 100 years, Herod the Great and his descendants played prominent roles in Israel's history. When Herod the Great died, his kingdom was divided between three of his sons. Throughout the gospels and the book of Acts, the Herod family is connected to key biblical events.

HEROD THE GREAT

Herod the Great reigned over the land of Israel during the time when Jesus was born. At that time, Israel was not free, but was under the domination of the powerful Roman Empire. Herod the Great's authority to rule over Israel was given to him by the Roman Empire and he was subordinate to their commands.

Herod the Great is remembered in history for his stunning and innovative building projects. He built Caesarea Maritima on the Mediterranean coast; its aqueduct and some other structures are still standing. Driven by paranoia, he built two mountaintop fortress-palaces – Herodian and Masada – in case he needed to escape for his life. Herod also designed state-of-the-art water storage cisterns and stone conduits to transfer water into Jerusalem.

But Herod the Great's crowning achievement was the Temple in Jerusalem. He built a massive and magnificent complex to support and surround the Temple. The Western Wall is a remnant of that structure. (Most of the Temple complex, along with almost all of Jerusalem, was destroyed by Titus in 70 A.D.)

2,000-year-old archaeological ruins still exist and serve as testimony to Herod the Great's building achievements. One day, as I was walking through Independence Park in Jerusalem, I noticed a huge stone reservoir. Turns out that this reservoir, called Mamilla Pool, was a part of Herod the Great's water supply system. It was linked to the Old City of Jerusalem by an underground channel. It measures 291 feet by 192 feet. It was designed to hold 30,000 cubic meters of water.

Another time, as we were walking through the park, a man sat in the (dry) reservoir reading a newspaper. It was a funny sight, but I suppose it was a quiet place to read, there in the ruins of Herod the Great's handiwork.

But Herod the Great's personal and political life reads like a bad dream turned into a horrific nightmare. Deceit, murder, and other abnormal behavior defined him and produced sour fruit on his family tree. He ordered the assassination of one of his wives, Mariamne I, and her mother, Alexandra. Two brothers-in-law died as a result of his insane behavior and paranoia: Aristobulus III and Kostobar. He accused three sons – Antipater III, Alexander, and Aristobulus IV – of plotting against him and they were also executed.

Considering Herod the Great's tendency to kill anyone he considered a threat to his kingship, it is not hard to believe that he ordered the death of innocent children, since he feared that one of them would someday take away his power (Matthew 2:1-20).

Herod the Great was not really a Jew. His father – Antipater – was an Idumean. His mother – Kufro – was a Nabatean. (History records that Herod the Great spent most of his childhood in Petra, that great Nabatean city.) Idumean was the Greek word for Edomite. Thus, Herod the Great and his descendants were actually Edomites.

Herod the Great's father was forced to convert to Judaism by John Hyrcanus. I asked a tour guide at the Israel Museum if she considered Herod a true Jew. She did not seem to want to answer but, without elaboration, she abruptly said, "If you've converted to Judaism, you're Jewish." But the Pharisaic traditions of Herod the Great's time did not consider forcible conversion legitimate.

The Jews of Herod the Great's time did not like him, not just because he was partial to Rome, but because they knew he was not really one of them. The word "Herod" is akin to the word "hero." But Jews did not consider him their hero.

HEROD ANTIPAS

This is one of Herod the Great's sons. After his father's death, he ruled over Galilee and Perea. (Perea is the area east of the Jordan River, in the modern-day Kingdom of

Jordan.) Herod Antipas is best known for ordering the beheading of John the Baptist.

Herod Antipas' first wife was Phasaelis, the daughter of Aretas IV, king of the Nabateans in Petra. Herod Antipas divorced Phasaelis to marry Herodias, the wife of his half-brother Herod Philip I. Phasaelis returned to Petra. Shortly thereafter, Aretas IV and his army invaded the territory of Herod Antipas, capturing some of his holdings.

Although history does not specifically say that Aretas IV's invasion of Herod Antipas' land was because he divorced Phasaelis, it is highly probable that Aretas IV retaliated because Herod Antipas had shamed his daughter and their family.

Because John told Herod Antipas, "It is not lawful for thee to have thy brother's wife," Herod Antipas put him in prison. At least on the surface, Herod Antipas liked John and listened to him, "and when he heard him, he did many things, and heard him gladly." However, Herodias was a wicked woman and, using her daughter Salome, contrived a deceitful plan to trick Herod Antipas into beheading John the Baptist.

During Jesus' trial, he was brought before Pontius Pilate. When Pilate found out that Jesus was a Galilaean, he sent him to Herod Antipas, since Galilee was within his jurisdiction. Herod Antipas happened to be in Jerusalem at the time and the Bible says that "when Herod saw Jesus, he was exceeding glad: for he was desirous to see him of a long season, because he had heard many things of him; and he hoped to have seen some miracles done by him."

Was Herod Antipas sincere in wanting to listen to Jesus? Or was he just interested in watching a show of healings and miracles? Earlier in his ministry, Jesus called Herod

Antipas "that fox." Perhaps Jesus knew the real intentions of Herod Antipas' heart and so "he answered him nothing."

This must have infuriated Herod Antipas, a man accustomed to wielding his power and expecting his commands to be obeyed. His initial gladness turned to wrath and he and his men mocked Jesus, placing on him a "gorgeous robe." He could find no reason to sentence Jesus, so he sent Him back to Pontius Pilate.

(See Matthew 14:1-10; Mark 6:14-28; 8:15; Luke 3:1,19; 9:7-9; 13:31-32; 23:6-12; Acts 13:1.)

HEROD ARCHELAUS

This is one of Herod the Great's sons. After his father's death, he ruled over Judea, Samaria, and Idumea. During the reign of Herod the Great, Mary and Joseph fled to Egypt to escape Herod the Great's brutal wrath. When Herod the Great died, an angel appeared to Joseph and told him to return to Israel.

But when Joseph heard that Archelaus ruled over Judea, the area that included Bethlehem, he was afraid. Then, "being warned of God in a dream, he turned aside into the parts of Galilee. And he came and dwelt in a city called Nazareth: that it might be fulfilled which was spoken by the prophets, He shall be called a Nazarene" (Matthew 2:19-23).

Herod Archelaus ruled for only two years before being banished to Gaul by Rome.

(See Matthew 2:22.)

HEROD PHILIP I

This is one of Herod the Great's sons. Herod Philip I married Herodias and they had a daughter named Salome. Herodias decided to leave Herod Philip I and marry his brother (Herod Antipas) instead.

Herod Philip I did not become involved in civil leadership. Perhaps his lack of political ambition is part of what motivated Herodias to seek a more illustrious life with Herod Antipas.

(See Matthew 14:3-11; Mark 6:17; Luke 3:19.)

HEROD PHILIP II

This is one of Herod the Great's sons. After his father's death, he ruled over Ituraea and Trachonitis, modern-day Syria. Herod Philip II rebuilt Caesarea Philippi in the northern area of Israel. He married his niece Salome.

(See Luke 3:1.)

HEROD AGRIPPA I

This is one of Herod the Great's grandsons. He ruled Galilee, Trachonitis, Perea, and Judea. He persecuted the New Testament church and is especially remembered for the murder of James and the imprisonment of Peter.

Herod Agrippa I sat on his throne and made a speech. People shouted and said, "It is the voice of a god, and not of a man." The angel of the Lord smote him and he died, "because he gave not God the glory."

(See Acts 12:1-23.)

HEROD AGRIPPA II

This is Herod the Great's great-grandson, the son of Herod Agrippa I. He ruled over Chalis, in southern Lebanon and was later given authority over other areas as well. Rome issued to Herod Agrippa II the oversight of the temple in Jerusalem, and he was authorized to appoint the high priest.

Paul was being accused of the Jews when he was transferred to Caesarea Maritima for judgment before Felix, the governor of Judah. Felix was married to Drusilla, the daughter of Herod Agrippa I. They listened to Paul, and "Felix, trembled, and answered, Go thy way for this time; when I have a convenient season, I will call for thee." Felix was sympathetic toward Paul's plight and was drawn by Paul's words, but He never relinquished his will and became a Christian. He kept Paul in prison.

After two years, Festus succeeded Felix as governor. He brought Paul before him for trial and Paul was again accused by the Jews. During this time, Herod Agrippa II and his sister Bernice came to visit Festus in Caesarea Maritima. Herod Agrippa II decided to hear Paul himself. Paul described his conversion and concluded his statements with a gripping question directed to Herod Agrippa II. "King Agrippa, believest thou the prophets? I know that thou believest. Then Agrippa said unto Paul, Almost thou persuadest me to be a Christian."

History tells us that Herod Agrippa II had been raised and educated in Rome. So his sympathies must have favored Rome rather than the Jews, for, during the Jewish rebellion against Rome, he sided with Rome. After Jerusalem was destroyed by Titus in 70 A.D., Herod Agrippa II returned unscathed to Rome, where he lived out the rest of his days.

(See Acts 23-26.)

FOUR GENERATIONS – MANY OPPORTUNITIES

Herod Agrippa II was the last member of the Herodian dynasty. Four generations of his family had been in direct contact with opportunities to welcome and embrace the Messiah. Herod the Great could have met baby Jesus, but he tried to destroy Him instead. Herod Antipas had personal audiences with John the Baptist. Herod Agrippa I chose to persecute the new church. And Herod Agrippa II was taught by the great apostle Paul.

So many opportunities to turn a dysfunctional, mixed-up family into something good. So much rejection of the one thing that could help them.

So here may be a clue as to why the Herodian dynasty was filled to overflowing with not just political intrigue, but personal moral failure of the worst kind. When they converted, it was a political necessity. It was not a heart conversion. They did not – from the heart – serve the One True God of Israel. Inside, they did not change...even when they encountered Jesus the Messiah – the best Jew of all.

The Golan Heights

In 1973, Syria from the Northeast and Egypt from the South, backed by other Arab countries, invaded Israel on Yom Kippur, the Day of Atonement. They took advantage of the one day of the year when nearly all Israelis would be indoors, resting, fasting, and praying. Many soldiers left their posts to spend the day with their families. Public transportation and broadcasting were shut down in observance of that day.

However, some analysts believe that the surprise attack was to the Israelis' advantage. The roads were clear to mobilize forces and broadcasting was free to focus the public's attention on the conflict. The war lasted just under three weeks, from October 6 to October 25. In the end, Israel resisted the invasion and pushed back the Arab forces.

We visited Mount Bental in the Golan Heights, a strategic military point. During the 1967 Six Day War, Israel took the Golan Heights from Syria. As Syria tried to invade and overrun the land during the Yom Kippur War of 1973, the Israelis defended Mount Bental and the area around it. The Syrians had approximately 1,500 tanks to Israel's 160 and 1,000 artillery pieces to Israel's 60. The battle was brutal and casualties were high but in the end, Israel still controlled the Golan Heights.

Between Mount Bental and Mount Hermon is Kuneitra Valley. This long, now-placid stretch of land came to be called the Valley of Tears, due to the casualties suffered as a result of the 1973 conflict.

The Israelis overtook the Syrian town of Kuneitra during the war in the most interesting way. On the final day of the war, a Syrian broadcast announced that Kuneitra, the Syrian headquarters for the area, had fallen to the Israelis. It had not, but the Syrian soldiers did not know that, so they retreated further into Syria. The Israelis then captured Kuneitra without a fight. A ceasefire was called and the Yom Kippur War officially came to an end. The abandoned remains of Kuneitra lay in a demilitarized zone between the two nations.

We walked through the old bunkers and trenches on top of Mount Bental, some of them pockmarked, mute and sobering reminders of the blood that was shed in this area in recent decades.

In the Old Testament, the Golan Heights region was referred to as Bashan. During Roman times, a province of the Golan Heights region came to be called by the Greek name Batanaea. This word was a direct reflection of the more ancient word "Bashan" that was used in the Old Testament.

Some scholars believe that "Bashan" refers to "soft, fertile, fruitful" land. This definition is certainly fitting. The area is lush and verdant, ideal soil for cattle and agriculture. About one-third of Israel's fresh water supply originates in the Golan Heights region.

The Bible contains several anthropomorphic references to Bashan. Ezekiel 39:18 refers to people as rams, lambs, goats, bullocks, "all of them fatlings of Bashan." David, in describing his distress, said, "Many bulls have compassed me: strong bulls of Bashan have beset me round" (Psalm 22:12). We saw a lot of cattle in the Golan and Galilee regions, making it easy to visualize these Scriptural analogies.

This area was heavily forested during Bible times and was particularly known for its oak trees. (See Isaiah 2:13; Ezekiel 27:6; Zechariah 11:2.)

Absalom was the son of David and Maachah. Maachah was the daughter of Talmai, the king of Geshur, a city-state located somewhere in the Golan. When Absalom killed his half-brother Amnon, he fled to Geshur, finding safety among his mother's family. For three years he lived there, until David called him back to Jerusalem. (See II Samuel 3:3; 13:28-38.)

The phrase "Golan in Bashan" is mentioned several times in Scripture. It was a city of refuge (Joshua 21:27).

Interestingly, Paul's dramatic encounter with the Lord on the Damascus Road is traditionally believed to be in Kokab, a village to the northeast of Kuneitra.

During the days of Moses and Joshua, the land of Bashan was known as "the land of giants." Og, a giant himself, was the king of Bashan (Deuteronomy 3:1-13). The children of Israel conquered Bashan, which God then allotted to the half-tribe of Manasseh (Joshua 13:29-31).

The boundaries of the biblical land of Bashan roughly correlate to what is today called the Golan Heights. From Mount Hermon in the north to the Yarmouk River in the south, Bashan is the land east of the Jordan River and the Sea of Galilee.

The view from the top of Mount Bental is amazing. On a clear day the observant eye can see far into the distance: Syria, the far-reaching Golan Plateau, and the Galilee region. If Mount Hermon was not projecting into the landscape, Lebanon would also be visible. A weathered signpost points to regional cities – Damascus, Amman, Baghdad – and tells the distance to those places. A United Nations compound in the valley is easily observed. It is there to maintain the sometimes volatile, paper-thin relationship between Israel and Syria.

On top of Mount Bental, it is easy to understand why the Israelis fought so hard to retain the Golan Heights. This is a formidable mountain range, a natural defense barrier, a protective wall. The Golan Heights are towering mountains of rock which rise steeply and immediately from the valley floor, 3,000 feet above sea level.

I am a far cry from a military analyst, but after seeing the terrain, I presume that whoever holds the Golan also controls the area around it. In the minds of the descendants of Abraham, to whom God promised this land, the strategically located Golan Heights is worth dying for.

Tip for the Traveler

If you go to Mount Bental in your own vehicle, leave early and plan to make it a day trip. I recommend packing a picnic lunch, since there are few restaurants in the area. Highway 98 follows the Golan Heights all the way to Mount Hermon. Two must-see biblical sites in the area are Tel Dan and Caesarea Philippi, which is today called Banias.

The Seat of Moses

The entire 23rd chapter of Matthew relates Jesus' scathing denunciation of the hypocrisy of the religious leaders of His day. He began by saying, "The scribes and the Pharisees sit in Moses' seat." "Moses' Seat" was both a literal and symbolic term.

In the synagogue ruins of Chorazin, in the Galilee, is a replica of a Seat of Moses. It is a rather small stone seat embellished with a simple flower motif and an inscription. The original Seat of Moses is stored in Jerusalem's Israel Museum. Discovered in 1926, it dates to the 3rd or 4th century A.D., but is probably similar to what would have been used during Jesus' time. A rabbi, synagogue elder or distinguished guest would sit in Moses' Seat as he explained the Scriptures. It was a special place of honor.

The law of Moses was read in synagogues every Sabbath day. "Moses of old time hath in every city them that preach him, being read in the synagogues every sabbath day" (Acts 15:21).

When Jesus returned to Nazareth, his hometown, "as his custom was, he went into the synagogue on the sabbath day, and stood up for to read" (Luke 4:16-32). On this particular occasion, after he read from the prophet Isaiah, "he closed the book, and he gave it again to the minister, and sat down." This verse is an example of how the rabbi or guest speaker would most likely stand when reading the Law. Then, he would sit while he expounded upon what he had just read.

Scribes and Pharisees were interpreters and teachers of the law of Moses. Their job was to help people apply the law to their lives in a way relevant to their current society.

The time of Jesus was approximately *two thousand years* removed from Moses and the law. When the law was given, the children of Israel lived a semi-nomadic life in the desert. After 400 years of slavery, these people were struggling to adapt to their new identity as a free nation. God provided them with laws to help them govern their new nation, interact with one another, and make proper decisions.

Conversely, during Jesus' time, the children of Israel dwelt in their Promised Land, but they were not a free nation; they were dominated by the powerful Roman Empire. Greek and Roman ideology influenced their lives. Their lifestyle was different from that of their predecessors.

Some of Moses' laws must have seemed archaic and unnecessary to people living in such a progressive society. Because of culture shift and modernity, people might have had difficulty understanding why it was important for them to observe such ancient laws.

That is where the scribes and Pharisees came in. While common men worked as farmers, carpenters, stonemasons, and merchants, the scribes and Pharisees spent a lot of time learning the law so they could teach it to those busy with other jobs. Using very old laws as their guide, they were to instruct people how to please God with their day-to-day lives and relationships.

The word of God is timeless. God does not change. His ways are right, regardless of society, culture, language, ethnicity, economics, or government. Biblical principles can be applied to any situation because human nature has always been and always will be the same.

The Mosaic law was designed to create a society that honored God as King and His laws as correct in every situation. So, while Moses' law might have seemed ancient and irrelevant to the people of Jesus' day, it was superior to every other ideology that tried to influence them.

Simply speaking, God's laws always work. When applied, they create harmonious relationships and a civil, orderly society. God's government is better than socialism, communism, an autocracy, dictatorship, or monarchy. It is even superior to democracy. It is God's ideas, not man's, that are effective at creating a healthy society.

In Exodus 18, we see Moses resolving conflicts between people and teaching them how to apply God's decrees to their particular situations. When Jesus said, "The scribes and the Pharisees sit in Moses' seat," He was saying that they were authorized to help the people properly apply the Word of God to their lives, as Moses did.

Conflict occurred when the scribes and Pharisees took it upon themselves to exceed simple explanation and application of the law. The rabbis called their traditions "halacha" and used them as a fence to protect the law. But often the fence replaced the law. They taught man-created traditions that had no basis in the written Word of God, either outright or implied.

These traditions had been passed down word-of-mouth from generation to generation. The Pharisees held them as equal to the written law of Moses. These oral traditions were additions to the law of Moses, and these additions – as well as hypocrisy – are what Jesus took issue with.

Jesus did not condemn everything the Pharisees did. For example, in Matthew 23:23, He tells the Pharisees that they should continue tithing, but he reprimands them for neglecting "weightier matters of the law, judgment, mercy, and faith."

The admonition "Woe unto you, scribes and Pharisees, hypocrites" appears eight times in the gospels (Matthew 23:13-15,23,25,27,29; Luke 11:44). The word "hypocrite" is derived from the word "feign," to be a pretender, an actor, as when a man projects an image different from who he really is.

The Pharisees were so consumed with appearances and protocol that they missed out on some foundational principles from the Word of God. They failed to grasp the true meaning of humility and the real essence of worship.

In a familiar example, found in Matthew 15, the scribes and Pharisees asked Jesus, "Why do thy disciples transgress the tradition of the elders? for they wash not their hands when they eat bread." Jesus responded, "Why do ye also transgress the commandment of God by your tradition?"

Here we see a clash between the "tradition of the elders" and the "commandment of God." Several times Jesus berated the scribes and Pharisees for following the "tradition of the elders" and the "tradition of men." These were self-imposed laws that Jesus did not expect people to adhere to. Jesus told them, "Ye made the commandment of God of none effect by your tradition."

In an appeal to help the Pharisees understand how blind they were, Jesus referenced the prophet Isaiah: "This people draweth nigh unto me with their mouth, and honoureth me with their lips; but their heart is far from me. But in vain they do worship me, teaching for doctrines the commandments of men" (Isaiah 29:13; Matthew 15:8-9).

It is possible to put things on ourselves that even Jesus does not require of us. In our achievement-oriented society that values intellect, education, and success, we sometimes transfer that mentality to living for God. We behave as though we believe, "The more I do, the better I am." We tend to think that the more we do for God, the happier He will be with us.

If we live our lives only doing things for God, we are little better than the Pharisees. While God does expect us to be busy with His work, He places greater value on our character development, how we treat people, and inner cleanliness.

It is possible to be so good at *doing* that we stop *being*. We can become so concerned with doing things for God that we cease to know God. Or, our relationship with God is not as deep as it could be. It is gratifying to do things, to be busy with kingdom work. There is a time and place for work, but worship should be the yearning of our heart.

A fulfilling relationship is not one motivated by duty or service alone, although those are essential principles in the Word of God that should not be neglected. A fulfilling relationship is one that is motivated by a desire to know God, to draw close to Him, to give ourselves to Him.

In the New Covenant that Jesus established, there are still things God requires of us, yet we need to make sure we do not confuse self-imposed traditions or workaholic-style acts of service with quality of relationship.

As our relationship with God deepens, we will be naturally motivated to do things for Him. As we grow in the knowledge of His love for us, service will become second nature to us, not a chore or a means to gain His approval.

Living for God is simple. It only becomes complicated when we lose focus of what is most important. Jesus spent a lot of his earthly ministry simplifying what people had complicated. Jesus said, "Thou shalt love the Lord thy God with all thy heart, and with all thy soul, and with all thy mind. This is the first and great commandment. And the second is like unto it, Thou shalt love thy neighbour as thyself. On these two commandments hang all the law and the prophets" (Matthew 22:37-39).

There it is in a nutshell, plain and simple: a principle that is powerful enough to be applied to every situation in our lives. Micah 6:8 also says it well: "He hath shewed thee, O man, what is good; and what doth the LORD require of thee, but to do justly, and to love mercy, and to walk humbly with thy God?"

The focus here is on how we walk before God and how we treat other people. This is the crux of the gospel message. Loving God should become a *being*; it should define who we are and naturally motivate us to *do*.

At the end of life, if we have kept our priorities in focus throughout life, our relationship with God will sustain us. I have met elderly people who, due to failing health, were unable to give home Bible studies or prepare food for church dinners. They did not have the strength to dance before the Lord or lift their voices in loud praise.

But they had something deep with God that they had been cultivating for years. They had spent a lifetime depositing, not just service, but heartfelt devotion, prayer, and deep worship into their bank account with God. When they could no longer receive gratification from *doing*, their relationship with God sustained them.

Jesus constantly dealt with heart issues; He liked to get to the root of the problem. While Jesus did not necessarily condemn exteriors – unless they had no basis in God's laws – He wanted the Pharisees to look a little deeper.

Jesus wanted people to see past what others could see and past what they themselves normally saw. He wanted them to see themselves as He saw them. He told them who He was and He wanted them to know who they really were. Jesus desired for them to cultivate honesty and a deeper awareness of true reality.

Tip for the Traveler

If you visit Chorazin, ask the park attendant to direct you to the synagogue. You will see the Seat of Moses replica against one of the walls. Sit in it to get an idea of how petite the people must have been in Israel 2,000 years ago!

Chorazin is a great place to watch hyrax (rock rabbits) sunning on the rocks. These Chorazin creatures like to hang out among the rocks to the left of the parking lot. If you like animals, you will enjoy watching these rock dwellers.

Not all biblical scholars are convinced that these are the conies of the Bible, but they generally agree that the two are at least nearly identical in appearance and behavior. "Coney" is an antiquated English word for the Hebrew word "shaphan," which means "the hider." These creatures are quiet and easily alarmed. Get too close to them and they will dart out of sight among the rocks.

Proverbs 30:24 says that conies are "exceeding wise." "The conies are but a feeble folk, yet make they their houses in the rocks" (Proverbs 30:26).

Note: Watch out for lizards and snakes. They like the rocks too!

Additional Tip: If you are in your own vehicle, you can easily see Chorazin, Capernaum, and Bethsaida all in one day, since these three biblical cities are close to each other.

Aramaic

In Syria is a small village called Ma'loula. It is one of the few places in the world where you can hear people speaking Aramaic. This ancient Semitic language is related to Hebrew. It is considered an endangered language since so few people still speak it.

Most linguistic and biblical scholars agree that Jesus spoke this language. "The towns of Nazareth and Capernaum, where Jesus lived, were primarily Aramaic-speaking communities."[1] For several hundred years, including the time during which Jesus lived, the Aramaic language dominated the areas of Galilee and Samaria, where Jesus spent most of his time. Hebrew and Greek were also spoken, but Aramaic appears to have been the most common day-to-day language of Jesus' day.

The New Testament was written in Greek, but several phrases have been preserved as they were originally spoken in Aramaic. Here are some examples: "Maranatha" is Aramaic for "Our Lord is Coming" (I Corinthians 16:22). To a deaf man, Jesus said, "Ephphatha." This means, "Be opened" (Mark 7:34). When Jesus was on the cross, He cried out "Eli, Eli, lama sabachthani?" (Matthew 27:46). This means, "My God, my God, why hast thou forsaken me?"

To the little girl who was dead, Jesus said, "Talitha cumi." This means, "Young girl, arise" (Mark 5:41). As I was studying this phrase, I excitedly recalled a monument I had seen just a couple of blocks away from our apartment in Jerusalem at the intersection of King George and Ben Yehuda Streets. The monument is the original façade of a girls orphanage and school that operated on King George Street from 1868-1948. (Eventually, in 1980, the building was demolished.) Over an arched doorway was the name of the orphanage: Talitha Kumi. The name was no doubt thoughtfully chosen to hearten young girls as they entered the building with the hope of improving their lives. How wonderful that this beautiful Aramaic phrase with its message of hope has been preserved in the center of modern Jerusalem!

Some place names are uniquely Aramaic, most notably Gethsemane, which means "Oil Press" (Matthew 26:36; Mark 14:32) and Golgotha, which means "Place of a Skull" (Matthew 27:33; Mark 15:22; John 19:17).

Even some people's names – such as Cephas (Simon Peter), Thomas, and Tabitha – were distinctively Aramaic.

Of course, as all languages do, Aramaic has evolved over time. I was not naive enough to think that modern forms of Aramaic would sound exactly like the Aramaic spoken in Jesus' time, but I wanted to hear it anyway.

We have a friend in Jordan who frequently travels north to Damascus, Syria for business reasons. He volunteered to take us with him during one of his trips. At that time, for security reasons, it was not advisable for Americans to tour in Syria. And, other than my interest in hearing Aramaic spoken, we did not have much of a reason to go there anyway, so we never crossed over. The closest we got to Syria was viewing its majestic purple mountains from the northern area of Jordan.

Aram was one of Shem's sons (Genesis 10:21-23). Modern Syria includes what was once called the region of Aram and historians seem to agree that it gleaned that name because it was settled by Aram. Aramaic originated in this area. Syriac is a form of Aramaic.

As I studied about the Middle East, I learned about a lady who works at St. Mark's Church in Jerusalem's Armenian Quarter of the Old City. (St. Mark's Syrian Orthodox church is one of two proposed locations of the Upper Room, where the events of Acts 2 occurred.) This lady, whose name can be spelled either Jostina or Yostina, speaks Aramaic.

During our stay in Jerusalem, we went to St. Mark's Church and I was pleased to find that Jostina was working there that day. A former 12th grade mathematics teacher, she speaks English and Arabic in addition to Aramaic. She has been living in Jerusalem for 11 years, serving as tour guide and caretaker. She told us that as she cleans the church she prays, "As I clean your church, clean my heart. Please my Lord."

I asked Jostina if she would speak some words in Aramaic and allow me to record her. She refused to speak in Aramaic, but volunteered to sing the Lord's Prayer in Aramaic.

She closed her eyes and folded her hands in a traditional posture of prayer. Her voice was clear and her prayer-song resonated off of the stone walls. To my ears, it was a mournful tune, but it was thrilling to hear the syllables and nuances of this ancient language.

The sounds seemed to resemble Arabic somewhat, due to occasional guttural inflections, but Aramaic seemed smoother, a little more mellow than Arabic. I was thrilled that I was able to hear Aramaic spoken, and that I did not have to travel to Syria to hear it!

Jesus did not speak English, or French, or Spanish. The language of His time was one far different from ours. As I listened to Jostina singing her prayer in this nearly-extinct language that day in St. Mark's Church, for a moment I allowed my imagination to travel back 2,000 years.

Oh, what it must have been like to hear Jesus tell His parables in this language, to hear him speak lovingly to little children, and how beautiful the words "Talitha cumi" must have sounded to the brokenhearted parents of a young girl. Aramaic...it was a privileged language, blessed to be used by Jesus as He transmitted His message of hope to the world.

The Place of a Skull

I come down one road. You come down another. We all meet at the foot of the cross.

The title of an old song is "The Ground is Level at the Foot of the Cross." At Calvary, Golgotha, the Place of a Skull, we are all the same.

When we understand Calvary, we forgive. When we view the blood streaming from a broken body, we love. When we hear the women crying, we have compassion. Calvary enables us to overlook faults, because love covers a multitude of sins.[1] Calvary is our greatest example of suffering, sacrifice, giving beyond what a human being seems capable of giving. Jesus gave everything. He gave all He had to give. There was nothing left.

"Calvary, oh what it means to me.
Since Jesus set me free, I think of Calvary.
Jesus' blood, oh what a cleansing flood.
He did it all, for me, on Calvary."[2]

Whenever I am tempted to lift myself up, I need to kneel down...at the foot of the cross, where the ground is level.

Part of me wants to look away from Calvary, pretend it didn't happen. I don't like to read the last chapters of the gospels that detail the trial, the beating, the crucifixion of this man named Jesus. It is repulsive. "We hid as it were our faces from him."[3] He was despised. We didn't want to look! What an ugly sight. Why did He do it? Why? Why? Why?

He did it all for me…on Calvary.

Tip for the Traveler

Two primary locations are proposed as the site of the crucifixion and burial of Jesus: 1) The Church of the Holy Sepulchre in the Christian Quarter of Jerusalem's Old City and 2) The Garden Tomb, just north of the Old City, beyond Damascus Gate and off of Nablus Road.

The Church of the Holy Sepulchre is the product of Queen Helena's supposed discovery of a piece of Jesus' cross. Six denominations share space in the building. To me, the Church of the Holy Sepulchre is little more than a tourist trap, although Orthodox and Catholic Christians would probably vehemently disagree.

At the Garden Tomb, the rock of Golgotha (sometimes called Gordon's Calvary) looks like a skull and was a known execution site during Roman times. A nearby period garden tomb matches the biblical description of Joseph of Arimathea's tomb, where Jesus' body was placed. The Garden Tomb, although not necessarily authentic, allows the visitor a much more realistic glimpse into what the crucifixion and burial may have been like. Plus, the garden is serene and quiet, a little island in the middle of bustling Jerusalem.

Proceed with Caution

In the United States, people install alarm systems for security. Other people use dogs to warn them of intruders. In the Middle East, people sometimes use glass.

High walls, made of concrete or stone, are built around homes. People imbed broken glass into the top of the walls. This serves as a really good theft deterrent, probably better than a sophisticated alarm system.

I have heard Pastor Urshan define the word "circumspect." He used the illustration of a cat navigating the top of a wall, as it exercises utmost care to avoid cutting its tender paws on shards of glass.

When we went to the Middle East, I understood his illustration perfectly since I often saw such walls. A cat would take a cautious step only after exercising conscious and deliberate forethought.

Ephesians 5:15 admonishes us to "walk circumspectly, not as fools, but as wise." The word "circumspectly" translates from the Greek language as "exact, diligent, and perfect."

In other words, as we navigate life's path, we must employ utmost caution. Before we take a step, we must carefully and thoughtfully consider the far-reaching consequences of our decisions.

Because of the repercussions that poor choices yield, there is little room for error. Sometimes, once a wrong choice is made and the damage has been done, there is little remedy. Even if the damage is repairable, recovery time will be required, our work for the Lord will be hampered, and our good name might suffer.

What am I talking about? Here are six examples that define the importance of being circumspect in our own lives:

1. Choosing to fudge numbers when filing taxes, only to reap an IRS audit, embarrassment, and the reputation of a cheater.

2. Binge shopping sprees – which you indulge in to distract you from life's cares – that ruin your credit and create problems between you and your spouse.

3. Cruel and harsh statements, spoken in anger, that damage a young child's tender spirit.

4. Repetitive negativity and faithlessness, which discourage those around you and keeps you focused on the bad things in your life, instead of believing in God and exalting His ability.

5. A few moments of sexual indiscretion that forever changes your life and the lives of your spouse and children.

6. Refusing to admit and overcome a bad trait – such as procrastination, lying, or laziness – which all produce varying degrees of fallout in our lives.

We cannot redo our actions and retract the words we say. This phrase says it well: "A moment of weakness, a lifetime of regret." It pays to walk circumspectly, to consider beforehand if we are willing to pay the price for our actions.

On an ordinary day, under normal circumstances, cats are finicky. But put them on the top of a wall with protruding glass and they will exercise extraordinary conscientiousness. They will walk slowly and gingerly to avoid anything that has the potential to hurt them.

As we walk this path of life, we will encounter many things that have the potential to cripple our spirituality. It is the work of our flesh and the devil to derail us from living for God the way we should. Yet, if we will rely on the strength of the Lord, He will help us make choices that will protect us.

When the Lord issued commandments to His people, He told them, "In all things that I have said unto you be circumspect" (Exodus 23:13). The Hebrew word used here for "circumspect" is "shamar," which means "to hedge about (as with thorns)."

The many implications of the word "shamar" include "to guard, to protect, to beware, to take heed, to preserve, to observe, to watch, to save yourself." As we walk circumspectly, our cautiousness will create for us a protective wall, ensuring our spiritual security as we live within the confines of the Word of God.

So, if you happen to be in the Middle East, as you walk through residential areas, look at the top of walls to see if you can spot a homeowner that is using this type of security system. We saw if often in Jordan, and I have read that other Middle Eastern countries use the same technique.

Also, there is an overabundance of cats in Jordan. When I would walk to the dumpster to throw away our garbage, usually several feral cats would jump out, startled. (I learned to back away from the dumpster and toss the garbage in from a distance so that the cats would not land near me.) We were often serenaded at night by cats screeching outside our apartment.

Although they are a nuisance, we did not mind the cats too much. Apparently, they are highly skilled at eliminating the rat population; we never saw one rat during our entire tenure in Jordan. They could not possibly survive. (And I certainly prefer cats to rats!)

The long and short of it all is that between the glass on the walls and the screeching cats, I received an unforgettable lesson in "walking circumspectly." It pays to think before we speak, to pause before we act, and to seriously consider the potential ripple effects of our decisions.

Royal Family Tomb

Behind the landmark King David Hotel, on a hill overlooking Jerusalem's Old City, is a first century B.C. tomb. Though Herod the Great is thought to have been buried at his fortress-palace called Herodian, authorities think this was the tomb of his family.

Which of Herod's family was buried here we do not know. It is not even with complete certainty that we can state this is where they were laid to rest. But it is fascinating to see a grave so intact that dates to the time of Jesus.

Though the inside of the tomb has been made inaccessible to visitors, we could walk all around it. Steps descend to the door of the tomb. What I found so intriguing is the rolling stone that would have been used to close the entrance. It is big, thick, and carefully rounded. Producing it was certainly not an express project, but one that must have been time-consuming and costly.

After a deceased person was placed in a tomb such as this, the stone would be rolled into place, covering the opening. Clay or wax was sometimes inserted between the stone and the wall to seal the grave. It was common for wealthy families such as Herod's to be buried together in caves or sepulchers cut out of rock.

Jesus was probably placed in a similar tomb, but He did not stay there long! Though the chief priests and Pharisees, with Pilate's permission, "made the sepulchre sure, sealing the stone, and setting a watch," Jesus defied the grave (Matthew 27:57-28:15). Human methods of burying the dead could not contain Jesus, for He rose from the grave just as He had said He would.

Now, as He was buried, so we are buried...not in a rock-hewn cave, but in baptism into death. And, as He rose from the dead, so do we rise to walk in newness of life (Romans 6:4-5). This ancient tomb provides much more than a peek into the past, but serves as a picture of the victorious life Jesus wants us to embrace!

Tip for the Traveler

To see this first century B.C. tomb for yourself, take King David Street to the King David Hotel. Directly behind the King David Hotel is Bloomfield Garden. The tomb is in the garden.

After examining the tomb, walk east to the edge of Bloomfield Garden. This will provide you with great views of the Old City walls. Directly in front of you is Yemin Moshe, a beautiful upscale neighborhood. If you have time, meander down the streets and enjoy the lovely flowers.

If you are really adventurous, you can continue down the hill to Sultan's Pool, which lies in the biblical Valley of Hinnom. To find your way back up the hill, simply keep the King David Hotel in sight as you climb the steps through Yemin Moshe.

Glossary of Terms

Acacia tree – A tree found in the arid desert areas of the Holy Land and Sinai. It is umbrella-shaped with gnarled limbs and fine, leafy branches. This is the shittim wood used to make the Ark of the Covenant.

Amman – Jordan's capital and largest city. Capital of the ancient Ammonites.

Anthropomorphic – Ascribing human characteristics to an animal, force of nature, or inanimate object. Also used in the Bible to portray attributes of God.

Arava Desert – A long north-south valley that runs from the southern end of the Sea of Galilee to the northern tip of the Red Sea. May also be spelled Aravah, Araba, and Arabah.

Archaeology – The study of historical civilizations by the use of ancient building materials, artifacts, and other material objects.

Ashkenazi Jews – Descendants of Jews from Germany and Eastern Europe.

Bedouin – Nomadic desert-dwelling people, primarily of Arabian descent.

Beth – House, House of. May also be spelled bet, beit, or bayit.

Calvary – Latin word for the location of Jesus' crucifixion.

Golgotha – Aramaic word for the location of Jesus' crucifixion.

Haredi – The most theologically conservative form of Judaism. Although Haredim (the plural of Haredi) themselves reject the term, outsiders refer to them as Ultra-Orthodox.

Hassidic – Movement of mystical Haredi Jews. Sometimes spelled Chassidic.

Intertestamental Period – The approximately four hundred year period between the writing of the Old and New Testaments.

Jordan – The country that borders Israel to the east. The formal name is the Hashemite Kingdom of Jordan.

Kefr – Village. May also be spelled k'far, kafr, kfar, and kafar.

Kosher – Jewish laws that serve as standards for food selection and preparation.

Lebanon – The country that borders Israel to the north.

Polytheistic – The belief in multiple gods.

Rabbi – Teacher of Jewish law.

Syria – The country that borders Israel to the northeast.

Talmud – What Jews consider the Oral Torah, or the unwritten law of Moses. The Mishnah was the first written record of the Talmud (c. 200 A.D.). The Gemara was a written commentary of the Mishnah and other rabbinic studies (c. 500 A.D.). The Mishnah and Gemara together form the Talmud. There are two Talmuds: the Jerusalem Talmud and the Babylonian Talmud. The latter is more comprehensive.

Tel – A hill, or mound, created by the presence of numerous civilizations. The different strata are uncovered for archaeological purposes.

Wadi (Arabic) – Valley. Can also refer to a dry riverbed.

Zionism – A movement that originated with the primary goal of establishing and maintaining a Jewish state.

Endnotes

THE JOURNEY
1. *Where God Was Born*, Bruce Feiler, Harper Collins, New York, NY, 2005 page 38

IRAQ AL-AMIR
1. Matthew Teller, *The Rough Guide to Jordan*, Matthew Teller (Rough Guides Limited, 2009)

JERUSALEM
1. http://home.earthlink.net/~ecorebbe/id45.html
2. http://en.wikipedia.org/wiki/Teddy_Kollek

A ROSE-RED CITY
1. www.jewishencyclopedia.com/articles/1752-aretas
2. http://www.janetaylorphotos.com/petra.html

BEN YEHUDA AND HEBREW
1. www.torahlawform.com/Documents/Hebrew_the_pure_language_of_Zephaniah_3_9.pdf

ARAMAIC
1. http://en.wikipedia.org/wiki/Aramaic_of_Jesus

THE PLACE OF A SKULL
1. I Peter 4:8
2. Song Lyrics, "Calvary," Brooklyn Tabernacle Choir, *Giving Him Thanks*, 1981
3. Isaiah 53:3

Bibliography

Arise, Walk Through the Land, Roy Turkington, Palphot Ltd., Herzlia, Israel, 1999

Biblical Sites: Jordan Land of Prophets, Fawzi Zayadine, Bonechi, Florence, Italy, 2000

Frommer's Jerusalem Day by Day, John Wiley and Sons Canada Ltd., Mississauga, Ontario, Canada, 2010

How to Walk in the Footsteps of Jesus and the Prophets, Hela Crown-Tamir, Gefen Publishing House, Jerusalem, Israel, 2000

Jerusalem Israel, Petra and Sinai, DK Eyewitness Travel, Dorling Kindersley Limited, London, England, 2010

Petra, Jane Taylor, Al-'Uzza Books, Amman, Jordan, 2005

Welcome to Jordan, Promo Skills, Amman, Jordan, 2008

Power BibleCD v5.2, Phil Lindner, Online Publishing Inc., Bronson, MI, 2006

www.bibleplaces.com

www.biblewalks.com

www.jerusalem-insiders-guide.com

www.jewishvirtuallibrary.org

www.smithsonianmag.com

www.wikipedia.org

Cover Photographs

Front Cover Photo:
Sylvia Ferrin walking in Zippori (Sepphoris), Israel

Back Cover Photos (From Left to Right):
~ Ketef Hinnom, Jerusalem, Israel
~ Symbolic Fish beside Door in Armenian Quarter,
  Old City, Jerusalem, Israel
~ Bedouin Tent Overlooking the Dead Sea, Jordan

Author Photo:
Bunker, Mount Bental, Golan Heights, Israel

Other Books by Sylvia Ferrin

FOOD FOR THOUGHT
A Healthy Temple for a Holy God

COOKING WITH WISDOM
A Collection of Naturally Delicious Recipes

To Order:

Email: sylviaferrin@hotmail.com
Phone: 314.440.3975